AWAKENING A LEADER'S SOUL

Learnings through Immortal Poems..

... I am the captain of my soul

GAURAV BHALLA

M<tivational PRESS®
LEADERS IN GLOBAL PUBLISHING

Published by Motivational Press, Inc.
1777 Aurora Road
Melbourne, Florida, 32935
www.MotivationalPress.com

Copyright 2017 © by Gaurav Bhalla

All efforts have been made by the author to contact the copyright holders for the material used in this book. The author regrets any omissions and will correct all such errors in future editions of this book.

All Rights Reserved

No part of this book may be reproduced or transmitted in any form by any means: graphic, electronic, or mechanical, including photocopying, recording, taping or by any information storage or retrieval system without permission, in writing, from the authors, except for the inclusion of brief quotations in a review, article, book, or academic paper. The authors and publisher of this book and the associated materials have used their best efforts in preparing this material. The authors and publisher make no representations or warranties with respect to accuracy, applicability, fitness or completeness of the contents of this material. They disclaim any warranties expressed or implied, merchantability, or fitness for any particular purpose. The authors and publisher shall in no event be held liable for any loss or other damages, including but not limited to special, incidental, consequential, or other damages. If you have any questions or concerns, the advice of a competent professional should be sought.

Manufactured in the United States of America.

ISBN: 978-1-62865-421-9

To Teachers...
and deeper learning
To deeper learning...
and deeper understanding

To all
committed to this
deeper understanding
and acting on it

So we may better serve
our own needs, others' needs,
our planet's needs

ADVANCE PRAISE FOR *AWAKENING A LEADER'S SOUL: LEARNINGS THROUGH IMMORTAL POEMS*

(CONTRIBUTORS LISTED IN SURNAME ALPHABETICAL ORDER)

Awakening A Leader's Soul: Learnings Through Immortal Poems reminds us that at the center of great leadership is great humanity. Traits like empathy and humility provide the insight and understanding you need to lead others well. Filled with inspiration and imagination, Gaurav Bhalla's book elevates the discussion around leadership in a way that can help transform how organizations train our leaders of tomorrow. The following lines from T.S. Eliot are a perennial source of inspiration because they combine the call to strive, to explore, and to experience, while at the same time keeping one's sense of wonder:

> *"We shall not cease from exploration*
> *And the end of all our exploring*
> *Will be to arrive where we started*
> *And know the place for the first time."*

Ajay Banga
President and Chief Executive Officer, Mastercard

Why not draw upon the immortal words of great poet-leaders to provide the insight and inspiration so many leaders are seeking today? Through *Awakening A Leader's Soul: Learnings Through*

Immortal Poems, Gaurav Bhalla has created a thought-provoking resource on *Soulful Leadership* for anyone looking to fuel their journey to make the world a better place. Personally, I find the following lines from Ella Wheeler Wilcox inspiring:

"How 'tis easy enough to be pleasant
When life flows on like a song,
But the man worthwhile is the man with a smile
When everything else goes wrong."

Bob Chapman
CEO, Barry-Wehmiller, co-author of *Everybody Matters: The Extraordinary Power of Caring for Your People like Family*

There is a reason why *Soulful Leadership* is near and dear to my heart. I have deliberately inculcated a sense of soul into my company over the past 42 years. It has become and is one of our greatest sources of competitive advantage.

Bill Crutchfield
Founder and CEO, Crutchfield Corporation

The world is full of management books – but none are so fresh and deeply thoughtful as this one. With *Awakening a Leader's Soul* Bhalla raises the bar for executive education. If leaders took its lessons to heart, not only would their businesses be transformed but so would they. With its wise counsel and many wonderful poems, this is a book to be treasured. Personally, poems have been my constant companions with favorites from many poets - Yeats,

Rilke, Hopkins, Shakespeare, Dickinson, Szymborska, Milosz, and others.

Betty Sue Flowers, Ph.D.
Distinguished Professor Emeritus
Global Strategy and Scenario Consultant

Few books help leaders journey within. This book does, in an exceptionally imaginative and innovative manner, through the wisdom of immortal poems. It holds up the poems like a mirror to enable leaders come face-to-face with their own humanity, and see themselves differently. I am convinced *Awakening A Leader's Soul: Learnings Through Immortal Poems* will elevate the discussion on how leaders shape their leadership journeys, and how organizations train current and future leaders. The teacher that has left a lasting impression on my leadership journeys is Deepak Chopra.

Dan Hoeyer
Founder and President, Leaders Excellence, Inc.

If there is one leadership book that you want to spend time reading in 2017, *Awakening A Leader's Soul: Learnings Through Immortal Poems* is it. You read, reflect, act and repeat all over again. This book acts on you as you act on the learnings from it. It grew on me as I read it, and once I was done, I knew it would live in my heart forever. I love it!

Prasad Kaipa, Ph.D.
CEO Advisor and Coach, Co-Author of
"From Smart to Wise"

The need for leaders with purpose has never been greater in our fragile planet. Purpose does not appear out of the blue - it is honed and refined through constant consideration of both the self and the world. Gaurav Bhalla's contribution to the leadership journey is to provide leaders with keys to unlock the doors to discovering purpose through poetry. This is not a text to be skimmed and jettisoned. Its place is next to every leader's bed where it serves as a catalyst for deep reflection and mastery.

My choice of poem (also featured in the book) is by Christopher Logue, and it speaks for itself:

"Come to the edge, we might fall...
come to the edge, and they came,
and he pushed, and they flew."
Professor Nicola Kleyn, DBA
Dean, The University of Pretoria, Gordon Institute of
Business Science (GIBS)

I love this book, because it's an uplifting and transformative journey. It leads the reader gently by the hand on a stroll from the uncertainty of her own day to day dilemmas to the profound comfort of trusting her wise heart. During the journey, *Awakening A Leader's Soul: Learnings Through Immortal Poems*, itself a model of the integrated self, helps the reader experience what it feels like to be a deeply satisfied, *soulful leader*. By the end, Gaurav's transformed *soulful leader*, confident and motivated, launches into her new big Monday Morning task: to transform her organization.

Elsie Maio,
Humanity, Inc/*SoulBranding* Institute

"I came to your shore as a stranger,
I lived in your house as a guest,
I leave your door as a friend, my Earth. "

Even such a modest accomplishment, presented by Rabin-dranath Tagore in 'Stray Birds' (1916), now seems difficult to aspire for in our complex, rapidly mutating world. Securing for everyone a life of dignity in a clean, safe and healthy environment, requires sorely missing inspired leadership at multiple levels. Gaurav Bhalla's latest book crystallizes this mounting concern over the lack of service undertaken with humility and sensitivity, as well as the absence of commitment amongst our contemporary leaders. *Soulful Leadership* emphasizes that a crucially important human-centered sensitivity underlies effective leadership; the book surely merits our most careful attention.

Ajai Malhotra

Career Diplomat, Former Indian Ambassador to Russia

Trustee-Founder, Health and Education NGOs

Bhalla recognizes that business leadership is about action and leaders are hired to *do something*, which inevitably requires *sacrifices and tough choices*. This is where his book impressively makes the point that today's complex world requires leaders that are rooted, self-aware and reflective. He presents a new narrative on leadership inspired by poetry so that leaders can better understand who they are, what they do, and how their decisions impact the world around them.

Harish Manwani

Former COO, Unilever.

What can the world's immortal poems teach leaders? Everything. Because, just as poems connect humans across time and space, their teachings connect leaders – also humans – to all that is relevant for them to lead across time and space. Which is why *Awakening A Leader's Soul: Learnings Through Immortal Poems* is an extremely timely book and immensely relevant to us personally. We believe in the power of *Soulful Leadership* and in the power of poetry to help us shape our business philosophy of developing an "authentic connection between nature, individuals, and the built environment." An old poem that we rely on is William Ernest Henley's Invictus: *Out of the night that covers me, Black as the Pit from pole to pole, I thank whatever gods may be, For my unconquerable soul....*

Chris and Marty McCurry
Co-Founders, Bark House, Certified B Corp
First to Cradle to Cradle Certified™ PLATINUM

Compulsively readable…just what the world needed. With the help of the world's greatest poems and poets, *Awakening A Leader's Soul: Learnings Through Immortal Poems* vigorously transforms the conversation on leaders and leadership by locating the wellbeing and prosperity of human beings and the planet at the heart of all leadership journeys. Brilliant. The poem that has sustained me in my leadership journeys is "If," by Rudyard Kipling.

LuAn Mitchell
Leading Woman Entrepreneur of the World, and
International Best Selling Author

Gaurav Bhalla has provided a valuable window into what leadership is, and is not. True, "Character Driven Leadership" always comes from within, not from without, and is best seen in times of adversity, rather than abundance. Leadership is as much about transformation and development as it is about personality, example or inspiration. Bhalla shows us that all of us can be great leaders, and that all of us can burn bright. What wings dare us to aspire? What hand dares us to seize the fire? My favorite poem that has always inspired me is Carl Sandburg's "Grass" – a three-stanza poem that expresses how we can forget the lessons of history...*the grass covers them*...and as a consequence, we are prone to repeat the mistakes that caused the destruction of the past.

Rob Posner

CEO, NewDay USA

Soulful Leadership, the main theme of *Awakening A Leader's Soul: Learnings Through Immortal Poems*, appeals to my intellect, but more importantly, it touches my heart. The main reason being that it captures the three key orienting principles of great leadership: insight, humility, and hard work. Insight, because great leadership takes a special kind of insight to know where to look, when to listen; humility, because leaders need wisdom, strength, and courage to get out in front and make the bold move when necessary; hard work, because great leaders don't live on mountain tops, they work in valleys. My treasured touchstone poem that captures these guiding principles, and is packed with abundant wisdom about *Soulful Leadership* is an Italian sonnet, "The Windhover," by Gerard Manley Hopkins: *"...Brute beauty and valor and act...the fire that breaks...sheer plód makes plough down sillion shine...."*

Dr. Arlette Zinck, Dean and Professor,
King's University, Canada

Activist Guantánamo Bay Prisoner Rights
(Omar A. Khadr)

Contents

The infographic provides a *butterfly's eye-view* of the book's journey. A color version of the infographic is also available for downloading on the book's website – www.soulfulleadership.world

AN INVITATION

PROLOGUE

How can anyone's welfare depend on such as I am?
Sophocles, "Oedipus at Colonus"

Once upon a time, the world was a simpler place. In that simple world leaders faced simple challenges, and therefore had to cultivate and exhibit a limited set of capabilities. King George V (Michael Gambon) reflects on this in the movie, "The King's Speech," when he informs his son, King George VI (Colin Firth), "In the past, all a King had to do was look respectable in uniform and not fall off his horse." Simple.

King George V was very good at that—looking respectable in uniform and not falling off his horse. Then, suddenly the radio—or the wireless—arrived, and the world became uncomfortably complex. He still needed to look respectable and stay mounted, but now he had to *do* more, and *be* more. He advises his son, "Now we must invade people's homes and ingratiate ourselves with them…We've become actors!"

Purists may jut their jowls at the above example because it is from the world of cinematic art. However, since life imitates art, it is only fitting that we derive key similarities between the dilemmas faced by the two King Georges and the leadership ideas discussed in this book. First, invading people's homes through the radio required the two Kings, George V and VI, to become bigger men and get in touch with their own humanity. Because, essentially, it was human beings with all their frailties (the movie was about a King who overcame his stammering) who were doing the invading. Second, it required them to seek out new teachers, because the teachers who taught them to look respectable and not fall off a horse couldn't teach them to be warm, accessible, kind, and neighborly on the radio. Lastly, and perhaps most importantly, the two Kings, George V and VI, had to search for wiser ways to successfully confront and manage conflicts they had previously not experienced, especially those within themselves. When a new and complex world forged by the radio revealed and pitted different aspects of themselves—monarch, human being, actor— against each other, achieving and maintaining internal harmony required learning new knowledge and skills. It also required humility and effort. Invading people's homes through the radio was palpably more difficult than mounting their trusted steeds. The Kings had to learn to keep their egos in check, deal with doubt and failure, and persevere. In short, as the world became more complex, King George V's and VI's humanity became disproportionately and substantially more important to their effective functioning as Kings than their kingliness.

Something similar is happening in the world of leaders and leadership today. Simpler times have departed, and they haven't left a forwarding address. We live in a VUCA world (a term coined by the US Army War College in Carlisle, Pennsylvania, USA):

Volatile – unexpected, unstable challenges of unknown duration

Uncertain – change is certain; degree, direction, and extent are not

Complex – an overwhelming number of interconnected parts and variables

Ambiguous – precedents don't exist; a world of unknown unknowns

Like the two Kings, leaders are having to *do* and *be* a lot more. And just as the Kings discovered, today's leaders are fast learning that it's not their "kingliness"—how they show up and whether they have all the necessary accoutrements typically associated with leaders—that determines their effectiveness in dealing with the myriads of complex and multifaceted conflicts confronting them. It's not even the smartness and brilliance of their minds. Or whether they've attended executive development programs at Ivy League schools, whether they believe in the Jack Welch way or the McKinsey way, or some other "Guru-of-the-day" way. That's not enough, and in many cases irrelevant. In today's volatile, uncertain, complex, and ambiguous world (VUCA), leadership success is a function of something deeper, something more enduring than technical knowhow and leadership skills. It's a function of the leader's humanity—who they are, what they stand for, what they are willing to fight for, and what they are willing to accept and endure. Because what's in the leader's head may be smart and potent, but what's *within the leader* that guides what's *in the leader's head* is even more potent, because it is wiser.

Accordingly, the most important asset of leaders is not the smartness of their minds, it's the wisdom of their souls. In "The

Symposium," Plato suggested that one of the greatest privileges of a human life is to become a midwife to the birth of the soul in another—a wiser soul to make the world a better place. Leadership, too, is a privilege. It has the potential to change the world and make it a better place. But for that potential to materialize, a significant shift has to take place first: leaders have to experience an inner awakening, a renewed sense of self-awareness.

To cultivate and nurture this inner awakening and self-awareness, like the two King Georges, everyday leaders need to augment their existing knowledge and skills by seeking out and learning from a new set of teachers. Traditional leadership training alone, albeit impressive, isn't sufficient, because it targets mainly the leader's head. Granted, talk of EQ (emotional quotient, or emotional intelligence) is widespread. But emotional sensitivity and empathy for others and one's own needs, is not the same thing as inner wisdom. What today's leaders need are teachers who can help them travel deep within, and reveal to them their own humanity. This book regards the world's immortal poems as peerless in this regard, hence the title, "Awakening A Leader's Soul: Learnings Through Immortal Poems."

The primary goal of an inner awakening is nudging leaders to reimagine and reshape their thinking on the nature and dynamics of leadership. This rethinking on the role and consequences of leadership should, in turn, guide leaders to adopt a wiser calculus on how they exercise their privilege of power and resources, and for whose benefit. This entire system, from inner awakening to a conscious desire to use power and resources to increase the well-being and prosperity of the greater many, not just the privileged few, is what this book calls "soulful leadership." Accordingly, the book's main goals are to acquaint readers with the idea and practice of soulful leadership, and encourage them to embrace its practice.

At this juncture, some readers may wonder if these goals—and hence the book—are relevant only for people holding traditional leadership positions in business, politics, non-profits, and other civic institutions. No doubt, this book is relevant for them. *But not only for them.* This book's themes and ideas are relevant for all individuals, or groups of individuals, who have access to power and resources and the opportunity to use them. From this perspective, even though parents, teachers, priests, and nurses may not be considered leaders in the traditional sense of the term, they are in fact leaders because they have the potential to use their power and resources for purely selfish gains, or to make the world a better place. Consequently, they, and others like them, are also an audience for soulful leadership ideas and behaviors discussed in this book.

Other readers may reflect on the book's principal theme, "soulful leadership," and wonder what lies ahead. After all, "soul" is an intellectually-charged, emotion-filled word. It evokes spontaneous thoughts of morality, righteousness, and ethics – good vs. bad, right vs. wrong, ethical vs. unethical. But this book doesn't deal with any of the above-mentioned pieties. This book is not about spirituality or religion, it's not a sermon on ethics, and it's not a monologue on corporate social responsibility (CSR).

This book has an unabashedly pragmatic focus: wellbeing and prosperity. Not just of the privileged few who control power and resources, but of the greater many. This book asks a simple, but extremely pragmatic and relevant question: "Is it possible to have a meaningful discussion on leaders and leadership without inquiring whose needs leaders aim to fulfill, and whose needs they sacrifice?"

This book says, "NO."

The principal passion of this book is scripting a new narrative for leaders and leadership. A narrative that obsesses less over leader's traits and decision making style, such as charisma and empowerment, and significantly more about generating wellbeing and prosperity, and overseeing its distribution in an equitable and responsible way. Because if it's always—and only—the privileged few who stand to gain and prosper, then the needs of everyday employees will always be sacrificed. Because everyday employees need the money, they will show up for work, but pass through the working day unengaged and uninvolved, their bodies present, but their imagination, creativity, and enterprise absent. Surely, leaders and leadership can do better than that.

The book scripts its intended new narrative of leaders and leaderships through several essays that address characteristics of soulful leadership, like in-check egos, the importance of doubt, and the value of perseverance. Though the essays are independent and stand alone, the characteristics they discuss are interlinked and intertwined. They work together and holistically. Two examples: "doubt" helps rein in the "ego" and keep it in check, while "self-reliance" promotes "substance, healthy risk taking, and experimentation." In this regard, this book is different from others. The various essays don't merely speak to a checklist of characteristics and values. They address a holistic system of reimagining the nature and dynamics of leaders and leadership. The characteristics work in concert, so paucity in one area can't be compensated by abundance in another.

Each essay is structured to enable readers to journey within, rethink and reimagine their humanity, and emerge committed to embracing and practicing soulful leadership. Each essay features poetry and is anchored by a preeminent poem written by such immortal poets as William Shakespeare, William Blake, T.S. Eliot, Robert Frost, Walt Whitman, Emily Dickinson, Jalal ad-Din Rumi, and a few modern poets worthy of immortality, such as Rainer Maria Rilke, Kahlil Gibran, Czeslaw Milosz, and Wislawa Szymborska. Briefly, the goal of the poems is to illuminate the value and importance of the soulful leadership themes of each essay in a way that can't be accomplished by merely appealing to the mind. An entire essay later in this book is dedicated to explaining why poems and poetry are peerless new leadership teachers.

I am acutely aware that an ideal pairing of soulful leadership characteristics and immortal poems is extremely difficult—if not impossible—to achieve. There will always be soulful leadership characteristics that readers feel should have been included, or omitted. Similarly, with poems; some readers may be disappointed at the omission of a poem, and others with the inclusion of one. My apologies to all such readers in advance. But disappointment needn't cause despair. The last section will suggest opportunities for readers to expand the journey that this book has started. There is room for more.

Each essay is also accompanied by a custom, hand-drawn sketch. The goal of the sketches is to offer readers a chance, literally, to float away. Pictures trigger our imaginations and send us on unanticipated journeys. And since one of the avowed goals of this book's journey is to help leaders reimagine their humanity, the sketches are offered as additional vehicles for augmenting readers' engagement with the primary themes of the essays, and with the essence of soulful leadership.

The essays are grouped into four sections:

- The first section introduces the idea and practice of soulful leadership. It makes a case for why today's world needs more of it, and explains how immortal poems can serve as a new set of teachers to help incumbent and future leaders embrace soulful leadership.

- The second section focuses on characteristics of leaders and how they relate to the practice of soulful leadership—who the leader is, how the leader thinks, and how the leader acts.

- The third section takes readers beyond the world of leaders to worlds that soulful leaders should engage with—people, communities, cultures, and the planet—if they are to make the world a better place.

- The last section is about "faring forward," because the journey is long and demanding.

So Krishna, as when he admonished Arjuna
On the field of battle...
Not fare well.
But fare forward, voyagers.
T.S. Eliot, "The Dry Salvages; Four Quartets"

The seeds for faring forward are sown throughout the book. At the end of each essay, readers are encouraged to *Think About, Talk About,* and *Act On* the essay's theme. Through these simple acts of thinking, talking, and acting on the various characteristics of soulful leadership, readers can, in their own sphere of existence, embrace its essential ideas and practice them in personally meaningful and relevant ways.

This prologue is an invitation to begin a journey. I hope, dear readers, you will accept it and stay till the end. The essays, every line of every poem, and the sketches are eager to say hello and share their messages of soulful leadership with you. Let's meet them.

THE JOURNEY BEGINS

Soulful Leadership: A New Humanity

If we have become a people incapable
of thought, then the brute-thought
of mere power and mere greed
will think for us
Wendell Berry, "Leavings, 2005,
Number 12"

This book is about soulful leadership. To understand it is to appreciate the dilemmas and conflicts featured in the episodes that follow. Inspired by real events, they typify what thousands of leaders around the world experience daily.

The Marketing VP of a cosmetic company gets a call from her former secretary, a single mother with one child. She has an upcoming job interview and would like a favorable reference from her previous employer. Her performance when working for the VP was a train wreck, to put it mildly. She earned consistently poor evaluations, was warned several times, and finally put on probation for 30-days. She left before her probation period ended, as she was diagnosed with cancer, and had to begin extensive chemotherapy treatment. She's still undergoing chemotherapy, but has started searching for a new job so she can support herself and her child. The VP wouldn't hire her again, considers her incompetent, and doesn't think it would be fair to foist her on an unsuspecting employer. Her former secretary needs a job so she can support her child and have health insurance.

The Director of a Japanese long-term care facility is in a quandary. There is a shortage of Japanese caregivers, and the residents don't like being touched and cared for by "Gaijins," foreign workers. He is pushing for robots to provide nursing care for the residents since he has not succeeded in recruiting extra staff. A robot resembling a cuddly bear was brought in as an experiment, but the residents were not impressed. They complained of feeling neglected and lonely; they wanted human beings to visit and care for them, not machines. The Director's mother is the most vociferous protestor against these experimental caregiving robots.

The position of VP, Global Strategy at a pharmaceutical company is vacant. The Chief Strategy Officer (CSO) is required to promote from within and is considering two candidates. The first candidate is a 15-year company veteran with an excellent track record. The second candidate is younger and has been with the company less than 5 years, but has excellent ideas for future growth of the company. If he invests in the future of the company and promotes the younger candidate, he risks alienating some of his senior, most trusted talent. If he promotes loyalty—the senior candidate—he risks losing an outrageously bright spark. To make matters worse, there is a hiring freeze. So if the junior candidate left, the CSO wouldn't be able to replace him. The CSO is confident that the senior person won't go anywhere, because his children are enrolled in a local high school.

The innovation department of a processed food company has developed new packaging for its flagship brand of pizzas. It has a friendlier ecological footprint than the old packaging, scores the same on future purchase intention, but gets a lower rating on brand image. The marketing team recommends sticking with the old packaging, even though it means the company will not achieve its sustainability goals for the year. The CEO has his doubts.

Profits at the Indian division of a global software giant are significantly down compared to the previous year. Global management asks the Indian CEO and her management team to implement aggressive and large-scale cost cutting programs. Employee bonuses and salary raises could take a significant hit, they warn, if costs are not contained immediately One of the committed cost items for the year involves setting up computer labs in three of the poorest schools in the city. The schools are chronically underfunded and are counting on the software company's gift. Unfortunately, the Indian division can't meet the cost-cutting demands of its parent company and fulfill its promise of setting up computer labs in all three schools.

All five episodes carry within them the potential for soulful leadership, which is defined as:

Purposeful leadership journeys that are guided by an inner awakening during which leaders work diligently and faithfully to increase the ongoing prosperity and wellbeing of not just themselves, but others as well—the organization, people (employees, customers, communities, cultures), and the planet (health and resources).

Whether the potential for soulful leadership inherent in each episode materializes, however, depends entirely on how leaders confront and resolve the challenges facing them. In each episode the leader has to act, and act unequivocally. The Marketing VP has to act on her former secretary's request—agree to give her a favorable job reference, or deny her one. The CEO of the Indian software company has to act on whether to respect or renege on their commitment to gift computer labs to the poor schools.

The only way the principal actors in the episodes can move forward is to commit to an action that requires sacrificing something, or somebody. The only choice they have is *who* they decide to sacrifice, *how much*, and *when*. They can sacrifice themselves, or somebody else, where "somebody else" also includes the planet (as highlighted in the pizza packaging example). Or, they can sacrifice some combination of themselves and others. For example:

- The Marketing VP can move forward by refusing to sacrifice her preference for "fairness," and sacrifice instead her former secretary, by refusing to give her a positive reference. Or, she can move forward by sacrificing her own preference for rigid fairness to give her former secretary a second chance, thereby increasing the latter's wellbeing and prosperity, even though her recommendation could potentially reduce the wellbeing of the company where the secretary is hired.

- The nursing home director, believing that robots are the future of nursing care, can move forward by sacrificing the emotional preferences of his customers, and his own mother (who is also a customer, but not just *any* customer), to fulfill his own vision. Or, he can sacrifice aspects of his vision and increase the wellbeing and prosperity of the nursing home residents. But what if he can't find human caregivers, no matter how honestly he tries?

- Leaders of the Indian software company could honor their commitment to gift computer labs to the poor schools by sacrificing a portion of their salary raises and bonuses to meet cost-cutting commitments demanded by HQ. Or, they could sacrifice the education and job skill dreams of the poor students to meet their cost-cutting commitments, and protect their salary raises and bonuses.

What's striking about this non-negotiable need for action is that there is no one right way, or best way, to act. Each of the leaders—the VP of Marketing, the nursing home Director, the CSO contemplating the promotion, the innovation and marketing teams contemplating the packaging innovation, and the CEO of the Indian software company—has a range of sacrifices which they can make and justify. Whether or not we agree with their justifications is irrelevant. Just as striking as the absence of right and wrong ways of acting is that *there is no rule book*. No unequivocal commandment, or edict, that says, "Do this." Which begs the question, who do leaders turn to for guidance? Where do they go to obtain approvals and assurances for their intended sacrifices? How do they know they have done the right thing so they can sleep at night, wake up the next morning and look at themselves in the mirror without averting their own gaze?

Ultimately there is only one place they can go to, only one well they can dip into, and that's what lives within themselves. It's their own humanity—who they are, what they stand for, what they are willing to fight for, and what they are willing to walk away from—that guides the *sacrifices* leaders make, and which determines who gains and who loses. The pattern of distribution for these gains and losses is the defining indicator of the presence or absence of soulful leadership. Soulful leadership is absent if others are consistently sacrificed to increase the prosperity and wellbeing of leaders and their inner circle, those who have privileged access to power and resources. Conversely, it is present if the pattern of sacrifices results in an increase in the overall and collective wellbeing and prosperity of the entire system.

Viewed from this lens, soulful leadership has the potential of transforming the world and making it a better place because it uses a sacrifice framework that is not governed just by the "brute-thought of mere power and mere greed" that Wendell Berry cautioned us against at the start of this essay. The world needs more of the humanity that gives rise to soulful leadership because the need for it is strong and urgent in all walks of life, from the most public (handling of crises played out on a global stage) to the most private (the regard we show for nature in the privacy of our homes). A small sample of examples that speak to this urgent need for soulful leadership follow.

First, crises that play out on a global stage routinely scream for soulful leadership. On April 20, 2010, the Deepwater Horizon oil rig, owned and operated by Transocean and leased by BP, exploded in the Gulf of Mexico killing 11 people and causing one of the worst oils spills in history. By the time the source well was capped 87 days later on July 15, 2010, more than 3 million barrels of oil had leaked into the Gulf, wreaking gut-wrenching havoc on marine and bird life—shrimp, fish, dolphins, turtles, pelicans—and over 1,000 miles of shoreline from Texas to Florida.

The explosive event severely tested BP and its CEO, Tony Hayward, and rewrote their histories because of who and what BP's top leader decided to sacrifice, and why. Contrary to majority expectations, Tony Hayward did not drop everything and make managing the crisis his top priority. He responded instead in ways that suggested he resented the accident as an unwelcome intrusion into his life. The scarring of the world in which he and BP lived appeared secondary. His gaffes and irresponsible behaviors that followed the oil spill provide rich raw material for a highlight reel on leadership behavior driven predominantly by "self-concern." Everything he said and did, beginning with the lament "What the hell did we do to deserve this?" to discounting the severity of the spill, "It's relatively tiny," to the Nostradamus-like prediction "The environmental impact of the spill will be very, very modest," to the grossly self-serving, "I would like my life back," revealed his sacrifice preferences explicitly: he was willing to sacrifice others—people and the planet—but not himself, or any aspect of his life. That he *made* time to attend a yacht race at the height of the crisis only lends more credence to this assessment. The pattern of sacrifices inherent in Tony Hayward's decisions were skewed in his own favor. But, paradoxically, his reluctance to sacrifice some aspects of himself for the wellbeing and prosperity of others eventually led to *him* being sacrificed; he stepped down and was replaced as BP's CEO.

If Tony Hayward were a one-off, we could parade him as an errant eccentric and crucify him in leadership seminars. Unfortunately, he isn't. Self-serving, egotistical leadership behaviors are widely prevalent in all institutions and in all sectors of society, private and public, profit and nonprofit, even religious. The media routinely features stories of "Big Me" leaders destroying organizations, jobs, and people's livelihoods. The leadership crisis that Tony Hayward—and others like him—epitomize screams for soulful leadership, for a new imagination from leaders that doesn't discount so steeply the wellbeing and prosperity of others.

Situations within organizations concerning everyday work life also clamor for soulful leadership. Two fundamentals, trust and work satisfaction, appear especially hard hit and can be attributed to organizations disproportionately sacrificing the wellbeing and prosperity needs of their employees.

- Trust and confidence in leaders and leadership is at an all-time low. According to the 2013 Edelman Trust Barometer, less than one in five respondents trust their leaders with their wellbeing and their jobs.

- Surveys by other organizations, like Gallup, show employee dissatisfaction and lack of engagement with work and the workplace is at an all-time high. Words like "soulless" and "dehumanizing" are used frequently by employees around the world to describe their organizations and work environments.

A new imagination and a new narrative are needed for fixing problems concerning lack of trust and lack of engagement with the workplace. Soulful leadership is that new narrative. With a human-centric focus that balances the needs of leaders with those of others, it has the capability to walk trust back into organizations, and revive joy and meaningfulness in work and the workplace.

Social, technological, and scientific forces that are transforming the way we work and live are also clamoring for a new leadership narrative, one that can be provided by soulful leadership.

According to the World Economic Forum, we stand on the cusp of The Fourth Industrial Revolution. Technologies comprising this revolution, like mobile supercomputing, artificial intelligence (AI), Internet of things (IoT), 3D printing, intelligent robots, self-driving cars, genetic editing, and neuro-technological brain enhancements are fusing physical, digital, and biological worlds, and in the process morphing fundamental assumptions concerning work and life, including what it means to be human. Regardless of the sophistication of arguments put forward by technology- bewitched gurus, there is no doubt that machines and machine intelligence will disrupt life as we know it today and skew power in favor of those who control these technologies.

Is it a time of great promise, or a time of great peril? That will depend on how the calculus of sacrifice inherent in leaders' decisions evolves in this new era. It can be a time of great promise if leaders put people first by constantly reminding themselves that the new life- and work-changing technologies are first and foremost tools made by people, for the benefit of people. However, if people are burdened with all the losses because their wellbeing is discounted, it could be a time of great peril. Regardless, soulful leadership will be at an even greater premium. Leaders of all organizations—business, nonprofit, and government—will be tested to ensure they don't sacrifice and merely replace the everyday worker with technological advances (i.e. the "brute-thought" of machines, as in Barry's poem) —such people as taxi drivers, check-out clerks in grocery stores, computer maintenance professionals, etc. who may not possess the means and abilities to retool and remake themselves on their own.

Finally, nowhere is the need for soulful leadership greater than in our relationship with nature. To paraphrase social revolutionaries and poets, like Erich Fromm and Wendell Berry, we act like "Gods" when it comes to nature. We consume and sacrifice nature, frequently indiscriminately and without restraint, and replace nature's creations with our own—those that celebrate us, our power, and our creativity (nature is creative too, often impressively more than humans). We human beings sacrifice harmony between us and nature to satisfy our endless craving for material things, for "having" and "possessing" more. Soulful leadership can help resurrect this harmony by encouraging a shift from conqueror to caretaker, from consuming nature to celebrating it, so nature too has claims on prosperity and wellbeing, and has a seat at the table when we compute gains and losses from leadership decisions. We need the planet for our wellbeing and prosperity, and the planet needs us. Soulful leadership can help propel us toward this goal of reciprocity and shared prosperity.

For soulful leadership to manifest itself, for leaders to exercise their privilege and power for the creation of prosperity and wellbeing for themselves *and* others, a critical regenerative shift needs to first take place within leaders. They must redefine their relationship with themselves, with others, and this planet so they can reimagine their humanity—who they are and what they stand for. Without this regenerative shift, soulful leadership will stall and sputter, and be unable to fulfill its potential of making the world a better place. This regenerative shift is the "inner awakening" that featured in the definition of soulful leadership provided earlier in this essay. It is also what the phrase, "Awakening A Leader's Soul," in the book's title represents.

This brings us to the threshold of an essential question: how best to trigger this regenerative shift, this inner awakening?

We shall not cease from exploration
and the end of all our exploring will be
to arrive where we started and know
the place for the first time.

T. S. Eliot, "Four Quartets: Little Gidding"

Sometimes we need to leave traditional shores and travel far so we can see and know ourselves again in refreshingly new ways, so we can come back home again and see it anew. Consequently, this book will eschew all temptation to recycle tired ideas in shiny new packaging. Instead, it will venture forward and travel to the land of immortal poems to seek out new teachers (new to the world of leadership education and training, but old to the world) who can create epiphanies that unveil us, enabling us to see and understand our own humanity in ways we hadn't before.

That's where we are headed next, to the land of immortal poems.

IMMORTAL POEMS: NEW TEACHERS, NEW INSIGHTS

In the very essence of poetry there is something indecent:
a thing is brought forth which we didn't know we had in us
Czeslaw Milosz, "Ars Poetica"

Why poetry?

Why travel so far from the world of management gurus, leadership case studies, and personality tests to the world of immortal poems? Because poets stand tallest among all teachers in consistently helping us make sense of ourselves, our world, and our place in it in new and insightful ways. Poems deal in eternal truths. *"They are news that stays NEWS,"* is how Ezra Pound likes to explain the power of literature and poems. Poets and poetry operate from a deeper level of consciousness and therefore are an invaluable gift, especially when we find ourselves stuck in life, screaming, "Who am I?" "What am I doing here?". So let's explore how immortal poems trigger an inner awakening and help leaders understand and reimagine their own humanity.

Earlier, Czeslaw Milosz informed us that poems take us places we didn't know existed within us. Finding these unexplored aspects of ourselves may be uncomfortable initially, but this new awareness is priceless, because it helps us see ourselves, the world we live in, and our connection with it in refreshingly imaginative ways. Often, as if for the first time. Percy Bysshe Shelley, the standard bearer of romantic poetry, considers immortal poems as indispensable teachers for triggering an inner awakening because, without them, we can't see ourselves. "Neither the eye nor the mind can see itself"—*unless* reflected upon something which it resembles. Like mirrors, immortal poems reflect us so we can see ourselves, especially who we are on the inside. This is invaluable, because we rarely see the world as it is, or ourselves as we are.

And yet the world is different from what it seems to be
and we are other than how we see ourselves in our ravings.
Czeslaw Milosz, "Ars Poetica"

The importance and value of journeying deep to become aware and know one's own humanity has been stressed by scriptures and spiritual gurus for millennia. The wondrous Kata Upanishad urges *uttishthata jagrata*—Wake Up! The Delphic Maxim advises "Know Thyself," and Socrates cautions us that "The unexamined life is not worth living." Sadly, most people are only vaguely aware of their coordinates on some of the most pressing issues surrounding them. Like Rip Van Winkle in Washington Irving's tale, they sleep through revolutions that have significant, and often irreversible, implications for their lives and the world they inhabit. This may sound like an indictment; actually, it's a simple observation of reality. Every day, numerous instances occur—like not listening, objecting without understanding, summarily dismissing others in meetings and social interactions, uttering words (verbal and digital) without full consciousness of their consequences—that suggest we are not fully awake, not fully present where we should be, and not fully aware of who and what we sacrifice even in our most routine decisions. The explosion in the volume of writing on "mindfulness," and the growth in seminars and workshops to help us achieve mindfulness is testament to these Rip Van Winkle tendencies that many of us display. And it's not just individuals, organizations and their leaders are also guilty of Rip Van Winkle-like behavior. Otherwise we wouldn't hear leaders admit (albeit sheepishly), "We were asleep at the wheel…we were caught napping…we didn't see it coming… we should have known better…we should have been more alert," when pressed to explain business accidents and reversals of fortune in press conferences and media interviews.

Poetry's work is the magnification of being.
Jane Hirshfield

Poems don't just reflect us, they also magnify us. One of the thorny consequences of this magnification is that we realize we are not just one person. Several of us have experienced this when caught in the push and pull of self-confrontation. When we hear a bazaar of voices in our heads barking contradictory commands, and become keenly aware of an absence of cohesion between head and heart.

The purpose of poetry is to remind us
how difficult it is to remain just one person,
for our house is open, there are no keys in the doors,
and invisible guests come in and out at will.

Czeslaw Milosz, "Ars Poetica"

Shelley too believes that poems surprise us by revealing multiple aspects of ourselves. "They (immortal poems) lift veils, and create for us a being within our being." One name, yes; one body, yes; one person in that body, no. Head and heart in sync; not always.

Multiple identities dwell and war within all of us, and leaders are no exception. Who leaders are, and what they stand for, is both dynamic and multidimensional. It's rarely as straightforward and static as a slogan on a t-shirt, "I am…" Staying whole and consistent is challenging for the best of us, but it can be infinitely more difficult for leaders because of the demands and sacrifices their roles and journeys required of them. This multiplicity of selves is critical because different aspects of ourselves—the aspect that wants to collaborate, the aspect that wants to play "Lone Ranger," the aspect that wants to listen to the data, the aspect that wants to act contrary to the advice of data—have vastly different consequences for who wins and who loses as a result of leaders' decisions. Consequently, it is vital that leaders be wide awake, alert to which aspect(s) of their "self" answers the door when circumstances come knocking and demand leaders to act firmly and unequivocally.

At the end of the day, only leaders who have made a concerted effort to shape a cohesive and integrated sense of their own humanity—who they are and what they stand for—despite multiple guests entering and exiting, will be able to provide a crisp and unambiguous explanation to the question, "Why did you decide the way you did?" We may not like their answer, but that will not faze them because given the context and circumstances, they know it's the best they were capable of. Perhaps this is all we can, and should, expect from leaders. That they penetrate the essence of every conflict and challenge diligently and faithfully, not with an "either-or" mindset, but with a keen desire to find a "third way" with full awareness of all aspects of their being, because truth doesn't reside at the extremes.

Consider the following exchange between Martin Luther King, Jr. and a reporter pressing him to align himself with the government's policy and abandon his opposition to the Vietnam War. Rev. King's response was as crisp as his inner awakening, "Sir, I am sorry, you don't know me…I am not a consensus leader…I've not taken a Gallup Poll of the majority opinion."

He even quoted lines from a poem by James Russell Lowell:

> *Truth forever on the scaffold,*
> *Wrong forever on the throne.*
> *Yet that scaffold sways the future…*

During his time on stage, Martin Luther King, Jr., played several leadership roles and launched several complex leadership journeys. He had a rich and layered understanding of himself, his place in this world, and his own humanity. His decisions to sacrifice himself or others were not driven by the rigid prescriptions of rule books, or the ever-changing expedience of public opinion polls, but by the abiding inner wisdom of his soul. There are times that he sacrificed himself and times when he sacrificed others, but his sacrifice decisions were rarely driven by blind unawareness. Instead, they were guided by an inner awakening, by a keen awareness of which aspect of himself needed to respond in the best interest of the *"scaffold that sways the future."*

By magnifying our beings, immortal poems also ignite our imagination.

To see a world in a grain of sand
And a Heaven in a wild flower,
Hold Infinity in the palm of your hand
And Eternity in an hour.
William Blake, "Auguries of Innocence"

An expanded imagination widens the options for action and encourages adaptation and improvisation. Imagination allows leaders to customize and tailor the teachings from immortal poems to suit their own unique situation and needs. T.S. Eliot informs us that *"poems always belong to the reader, never to the poet."* Readers always take the poem to a place where they want to take it, regardless of the poet's desire or original intentions. Once the poem crosses the threshold from the poet's pen to the minds and hearts of readers, it takes on multiple and unique lives and, depending on the mood of its readers, spawns a variety of inner awakening and self-awareness journeys. The plurality of perspectives that poetry opens to us is critical in helping leaders navigate their leadership journeys in uniquely compelling ways. They can look to others for inspiration, but rarely are they going to succeed by merely emulating others. Emulation is a flawed and imperfect strategy. Context is paramount, since conditions under which a particular leader succeeds can seldom be completely replicated.

The ability to deal with VUCA contexts and circumstances (Volatile, Uncertain, Complex, Ambiguous) places a premium on adaptation and improvisation. Smart minds, while undeniably an asset, are rarely enough to help leaders chart unique and compelling leadership journeys.

The mind is its own place,
and in itself can make a heaven of hell,
a hell of heaven.
John Milton, "Paradise Lost"

Integrating the needs of others into leadership journeys is an art form, and can only be achieved when leaders adapt and improvise by fusing their smarts with a sense of their own humanity. Artists—musicians, writers, painters, designers, and others—do this routinely. All of them know their art, the technical aspects of it. It's a basic requirement, the cost of doing business; without which they wouldn't be artists. But the leaders among artists, those artists who have elevated the quality and substance of their artistic journeys, also know something significantly more vital. They know what they stand for, and what they want their art to stand for. These master improvisers don't merely implement their art based on the rules in their head, they interpret their art based on a sense of their own humanity. They go beyond their own artistic needs, *and* integrate them with the needs of the audience *and* the needs of the moment. It is this integration of self-others-situation that enables them to deliver the essence of their art in uniquely spontaneous and personal ways. Or as Ella Zonis so eloquently explains it in her book on Classical Persian Music, "… *artists perform not according to the practice of theory, but according to the practice of practice.*"

Leaders, too, need to navigate their leadership journeys according to the practice of practice, so they can shape and mold the relevance and meaning of their navigation journeys to suit the needs of the ever-changing times in which they lead. Their mandate is not merely to extend existing histories, but also to write new chapters for future histories. The loving and wise guidance of immortal poems is invaluable in helping leaders fulfill this mandate—first by helping them become aware, and then subsequently by helping them to reimagine their own humanity.

We constantly hear a cry for fresh perspectives, for greater imagination, and for renewed creativity in virtually all areas of society. Achieving an inner awakening by learning at the feet of immortal poems, so soulful leadership can manifest itself, is a fresh idea, an epiphany. It is a re-imagination of leadership roles and the purpose of leadership journeys. Unlike conventional leadership training tools that work from outside-in, these new teachers—immortal poems—work from inside-out, thereby resulting in a deeper, more enduring consciousness of how the privilege of power and resources can be used for the good of many, and not just a few. This is, perhaps, the most compelling reason to integrate learning from these new teachers into the training and development agenda of current and future leaders.

Finally, there are two other visceral reasons why immortal poems are peerless teachers. First, they are the most generous, devoted, and forgiving teachers there are. They ask for very little, but give a lot. Even when all that we remember is a single line (To err is human, to forgive divine), a single word (If). Even if we can't remember any other aspect of the poem, or the poet who wrote the poem, they forgive and continue whispering their wisdom into the inner ear of our soul. Nelson Mandela, widely regarded as the father of post-apartheid South Africa and one of the most illustrious leaders of our times, isn't around to confirm whether he could recite William Henley's poem, "Invictus," verbatim. But we do know, through his speeches and other informal admissions, that two lines of the poem settled in him and became part of the core of his humanity. They sustained him through his long dark years in prison and transformed him as a person and as a leader.

"...I am the master of my fate
I am the captain of my soul."
William Henley, "Invictus"

Second, immortal poems are peerless teachers because they take us back to more innocent times, when we were children and just discovering our humanity. We are all born into poetry—all new life is poetry—and we grow up with it. Regardless of our cultural, ethnic, or economic backgrounds, some of our earliest memories are of poems and poem-like forms, like nursery rhymes. And even though we lose touch with poems and poetry as we get older, we never truly disconnect from its word rhythms, insights, and web of meanings. Poems live on within us, silently and invisibly. Subconsciously, we never really lose touch with their universal themes and their eternal truths. So, while answering a question with another question may be considered inelegant by some—unless one is Socrates, or a Socrates-like figure from other cultures—in this case it may actually be telling.

Why poetry?

Why not?

Have you ever, dear reader, come across a respected and truly admirable leader who did not have the soul of a poet?

THE LEADER'S WORLD: WHO THE LEADER IS…

EGO

I am not I.

I am this one
walking beside me whom I do not see.

Juan Ramón Jiménez, "I Am Not I"

Ego is a nuanced word. Different people mean different things when they use it. So it would be prudent to establish a shared context and meaning concerning how this essay intends to use the word before discussing ego's connection with soulful leadership.

A common tendency is to equate ego with self-esteem (or its poor cousin, self-image...the two are not the same), which explains the typical practice of qualifying it with adjectives, like "healthy," and proclaiming that having a *healthy self-esteem* is vital for leaders. No contest. A healthy self-esteem is crucial, and definitely an asset in coping successfully with the complex and conflicting demands of leadership roles.

But ego is not self-esteem. In many ways, the two are opposites. This essay follows Alfred Adler, one of the three giants of psychoanalysis (Freud and Jung being the other two) who founded the school of Individual Psychology, and uses ego as he did in his teachings. According to Adler, ego is akin to self-aggrandizement, a bloated sense of self. It is an aspect of an individual's personality that operates from the conviction, "I am the center of the universe." Individuals who harbor this conviction exaggerate the importance of "I" so they can feed their incessant craving for power, prestige, recognition, and for control under all circumstances, by whatever means.

"I am the center of the universe," is an illusion and a falsity with perilous consequences for individuals who harbor it, and for societies that harbor those individuals. Which is why, through the ages, scriptures, philosophers, and poets have encouraged us to dissolve this illusion by differentiating between the real "I" (the world of universal truths and our true self), and the false, little "i" (me, my, the world of egoism, and the egoic mind). It is the little "i" that is the root cause of the illusion, which is why the scientist-philosopher, Albert Einstein, called it "an optical illusion of consciousness." And we know what optical illusions do – they distort reality and everything contained in it. How we think, how we act, how we relate to other people, and how we relate to nature, are all distorted out of proportion and blown off course by ego-driven individuals. When this tendency is present in how leaders think and behave, it has disastrous consequences for the organizations they lead and the environments in which they operate. This is why the same wise teachers referenced above also advise us to work hard at shrinking our egos—the bloated sense of "I am the center of the universe." Our ability to confront reality, as well as our wellbeing and happiness, increase in direct proportion to our willingness to devalue and stop the rampaging little "i."

On the way home, I stopped.

Author Unknown

After years of studying and observing the nature and dynamics of ego, Alfred Adler declared that no individual is so rich in emotional and psychological assets to afford the incessant demands of an ego. Organizations even less so. Egotistical leaders suck the oxygen from an organization, leaving the majority of its people asphyxiated, because they think they are indispensable. This makes them a liability and an ever-present threat to the ongoing survival and wellbeing of the organizations they lead. This, in turn, makes "BIG ME (little *i*) leaders" the single biggest saboteurs of soulful leadership. Hence this essay is featured first.

First, ego-driven leadership is disruptive and distracts organizations from their main missions, which is to move the organization to a future where it, and the people associated with it, can be better off. Ego-driven leaders always need more rewards and recognition: more prizes, more awards, more attention, more admiration, and more confirmation that their views are right, and the list goes on. What's worse is that the fulfilment of this need is short-lived, since the need for "more" is a symptom of a deeper affliction of "not-enough." No amount of "more" is ever enough, or can ever be enough. Since catering to this essentially insatiable need is not the primary reason why most people show up for work, ego-driven leaders routinely play the "boss" card to reorient the organization's resources and attention to serve their own needs and priorities. They may do so overtly by literally letting people know who's the boss, or more subtly by engaging in control-oriented behaviors, ranging from rescheduling meetings at a whim, to making last minute demands, to arbitrarily changing the composition of work teams, to funding projects that advance their pet theories even when data and expert opinion suggests otherwise. These needy behaviors have organization-wide ripple effects that disrupt the established rhythm and flow necessary for a harmonious work environment, which in turn reduces the overall satisfaction and wellbeing in these organizations.

Next, ego-driven leaders have a tendency of suppressing initiative, since they are convinced they know more than everybody else. Consequently, they spare few opportunities to show off their knowledge by giving directions, expressing opinions, even when not asked, and telling people how to do their jobs: "I think outsourcing is the way to go," "If I were you, I would forget TV ads," or, "Our packaging stinks." Not surprisingly, since they prefer "talking and telling," they tend to be poor listeners. Their stock responses and interruptions—"I know," "It won't work," "Been there, done that,"—rather than encouraging an open exchange of ideas, act mainly as conversation stoppers. Over time, these behaviors have the potential of sapping initiative. After all, if "the boss" knows it all, and is always going to have the final say, isn't it more pragmatic to just wait and be told what to do? Sapped initiative is often the root cause behind why leadership journeys sputter and stall. Individuals who are repeatedly denied initiative will ultimately slip into a dull, zombie-like relationship with work, with the organization, and with their leaders.

Ego-driven leaders often constrict choices and narrow future possibilities because of their tendency to overestimate their own worth and value to the organizations they lead. Because they perceive themselves as "big" (big shots), often larger-than-life individuals, they often overvalue their own smarts and devalue what they don't know. Hence, they often fare poorly in forming knowledge-sharing collaboration and alliances. However, like much of everything else they believe about themselves, this too is an illusion. In a VUCA world (volatile, uncertain, complex, ambiguous), the competence and knowledge of a single leader, or even a handful of leaders, is rarely sufficient to combat the uncertainties and complexities that constantly threaten to upend leadership journeys. No matter how smart leaders and their associates are, what they don't know will always overwhelm what they claim they know. The hero model of leaders and leadership has severe operating limitations.

I would I might forget that I am I,
And break the heavy chain that binds me fast,
Whose links about myself my deeds have cast.
George Santayana, Lines from "Sonnet VII"

Beliefs and convictions that arise from limited knowledge can only act as "heavy chains," that "bind fast" (i.e. slow down and constrict) options and possibilities for future growth and wellbeing, as George Santayana advises above. These heavy chains that bind fast ego-driven leaders, whether they are chains of blind addiction to one's own opinions, obsession with being right, insatiable need for self-aggrandizement, or an unchallenged sense of "I know," endanger the survival and future wellbeing of organizations, on two counts.

One, exploration and experimentation is sacrificed in favor of "short-term" wins because winning today provides an adrenaline jolt for "BIG ME" leaders. Waiting for long-term wins is often considered unnecessarily tedious and laborious. This preference for short-term wins can make organizations more vulnerable to future market and environmental changes, especially if the next big opportunity for them to grow and prosper lies outside the tunnel in which the ego-driven prefer to search for wins.

Two, they quash dissent. Ego-driven leaders also have a strong craving for being right, and don't like being challenged. Since they don't like hearing bad news, they sponsor a culture of "sycophancy and political conformity," by surrounding themselves with "yes" people who rarely disagree and who meticulously feed them a daily diet of carefully filtered, agreeable information. What most ego-driven leaders don't realize, and acknowledge to themselves, is that political conformity, especially with the big boss, is a liability, never a strength. The absence of conflict it supposedly brings is attained only by sacrificing something significantly more valuable: an accurate and complete perspective of the organization's operating reality. It's like navigating choppy waters dotted with icebergs in a thick fog: accidents will happen.

Finally, and perhaps the most important reason, why leaders with bloated egos are champion saboteurs for soulful leadership is because they are inherently incapable of cultivating the fundamental force that drives leadership roles and leadership journeys—TRUST. It doesn't matter to which school an individual subscribes—trust is given vs. trust is earned—ego-driven leaders don't make it to the medal podium; they can neither earn trust, nor are they given trust easily, because people know that, regardless of promises, when the dust settles the ego-centered leader's needs will always take precedence over theirs. Even though both ego and trust are complex ideas, mathematically the relationship between them is simple: Trust $\propto$ 1/Ego. Meaning, the larger the size of a leader's ego (an exaggerated sense of self and a me-first mindset), the lower the trust.

Leaders, frequently ordinary people, are asked to play extraordinary roles. Hence they are judged by a different standard than the rest of us. Perennially on stage, they are highly visible beings and are expected to conduct themselves in an exemplary manner, which includes how they manage their egos and themselves. They are expected to demonstrate through their thoughts, words, and deeds that they are capable of becoming larger human beings, rising above their historical selves, so they can do justice to the role they've been awarded. For leaders to become larger human beings, for them to rise above their historical selves, they must first tame and shrink their egos, and walk away from the "I am the center of the universe" mindset. It's a prerequisite for the commencement of soulful leadership journeys.

Is there a poem that can inspire the commencement of this journey and encourage us to consider an alternative world-view to ego-driven, "BIG ME" leaders and leadership?

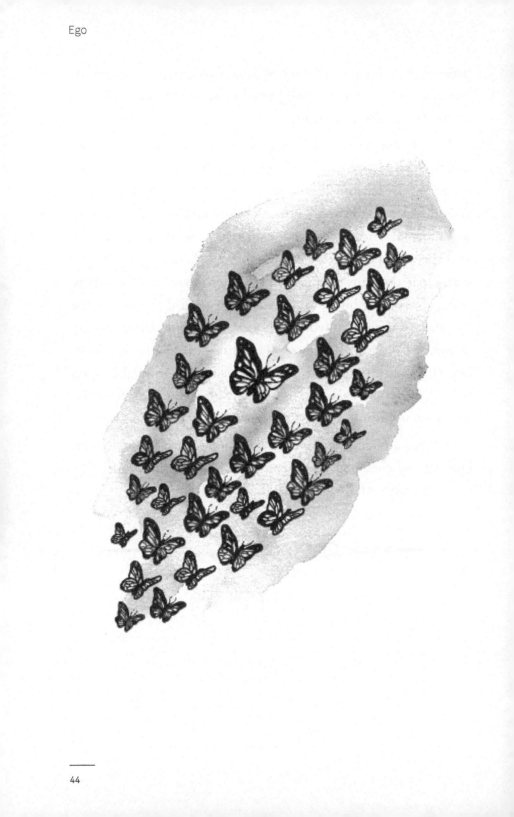

If "I am the center of the universe" is the overbearing characteristic of "BIG ME" thinking, then "I'm nobody" has to be its perfect foil. At a minimum, it offers us a diametrically opposite reality. What if there were a poem that did just that? That declared, boldly, and unabashedly, "I'm nobody." Then asked innocently, "Who are You?", thereby inviting us to reflect on the not-so-obvious implications and advantages of "I'm nobody" leadership.

I'm nobody! Who are you?

Are you nobody too?

Then there's a pair of us – don't tell!

They'd banish us, you know!

How dreary to be somebody!

How public, like a frog

To tell your name the livelong day

To an admiring bog!

Emily Dickinson

Is it possible for a person—a somebody—to be a nobody? The preposterous opening disarms us instantly. Even more disarming is that Emily Dickinson is not moaning being a nobody— "*Woe be me, I am a nobody*"—no, she's actually celebrating it.

And she is looking to surround herself with other nobodies, because being around somebodies can be "oh so dreary." Our own experiences confirm this; how often after an encounter with a "so-called-somebody" we sink into a chair and harrumph, "Boy, that person sure wears me out."

That's what the second half of the poem addresses, the oppressiveness of being a somebody. Being a big shot, despite what it may look and feel like on the outside, is often the opposite of glamorous and fun. Being in the spotlight, *how public*; always talking *like a frog*; saying the same thing over and over again in order to maintain a public persona of importance *to tell one's name—the livelong day*; never a moment alone, forever surrounded by a demanding crowd *to an admiring bog*, is a heavy burden for both the leaders and their organizations. What's worse, the symbolism and rituals associated with being a "somebody" sacrifice time and resources, and frequently distract and derail leadership journeys.

Across the globe, leaders are constantly exhorting their organizations and institutions to develop new solutions to customer and societal problems, to innovate and develop new businesses for fueling growth by "thinking outside the box." This poem is a provocation to think outside the box, to challenge our conditioned and conventional thinking about egos, and is an invitation to explore the sphere of soulful leadership by reevaluating the costs and benefits, the advantages and disadvantages, associated with being a somebody versus being a nobody.

Let's accept this invitation and for a few moments replace our protestations and incredulity, "How can a leader be a nobody?" with a counter-inquiry, "Why can't a nobody be an effective leader, perhaps even more effective than a somebody?" Imagine leaders who approach their roles—their work, their people, and their organizations—with an "I am a nobody mindset." Can you imagine how many previously excluded people it would draw into strategic conversations, how many topics, previously off the table, would now be discussed vigorously, how an enthusiasm for learning, experimenting, and innovating would replace the "I know," and "I think this is the way it should be done" orientations, and how it would make organizations even more capable of facing future customer, competitive, and technological challenges? Can you imagine the power of an "I am a nobody" culture in making work and the workplace more humanistic and soulful?

I am a nobody doesn't mean the leader is not confident, that the leader lacks knowledge, or is indulging in false humility. All it means and suggests is there is a new, viable, and effective alternative to the ego-driven, heroic model of leadership, one which doesn't require the leader to be the center of the organization's universe. Instead, a nobody model would encourage leaders to operate away from the spotlight and from the crush of admiring bogs so that the "I" can be replaced by a more enduring and powerful "We." The nobody model would also open doors to fresh ideas, promote initiative, and encourage experimentation, all vital for effective adaptation and improvisation. Above all, the nobody model would restore trust. All of this would add up to increasing the wellbeing and prosperity for all—organizations, the people who work there, and the leaders themselves.

It's time now to ask you, dear reader, how you (and your co-workers) can explore an "I am a nobody" mindset and promote an "I am a nobody" culture in your own organization and workplace?

THINK ABOUT IT

- Travel within and examine your own equation with the idea of being a "nobody." What aspects of it do you personally find appealing? What aspects of it have you wondering and questioning?

TALK ABOUT IT

- Talk about the power of being a nobody. Hold brainstorming sessions to discuss what it would look like, what it would feel like. Focus on a few specific areas and sacred cows, such as how people handle disagreements, challenges, and differences in opinions, especially when the parties have unequal seniority and power.

ACT ON IT

- Start small, start local. With the aid of your colleagues and superiors, institute an "I'm a nobody" culture in important meetings and workshops where bloated egos historically have disrupted harmony and productivity. Perhaps creating awareness will alone lead to different outcomes. Nothing ventured, nothing gained.

SELF-RELIANCE

Not I, not anyone else can travel that road for you,
You must travel it for yourself.
Walt Whitman, "Song of Myself"

We encounter the word "self" in a variety of ways and contexts in everyday life—God helps those who help themselves, Self-help books, and Trust yourself, are just a few examples. Typically, we don't stop and dissect how the word self is used each time we encounter it, because even though intellectually we may be unable to articulate exactly what the "self" is, intuitively we understand what is being said and implied. Just as in the two lines from Walt Whitman's iconic poem, "Song of Myself" at the top of the page. We know and understand exactly what Whitman means when he uses words and phrases, like "I...you...not any one else...yourself." So, technically, this essay could proceed without any formal explanation of self, or self-reliance – the focus of this essay—without fuss, or undue guilt. However, it wouldn't be seemly, especially since the previous essay focused on ego, namely, how an exaggerated sense of I trips up soulful leadership. At a minimum, this essay is obliged to pause and explain the difference between ego and self, before proceeding with its main message.

Let's return to Walt Whitman's iconic poem for context to explain the difference between ego and self. The iconic poem, "Song of Myself," is not a laudation of his stature as the center of the universe. It is instead a celebration of a larger consciousness of relationships between himself, others, and nature, in which he—Walt Whitman—the "I" in the lines above is merely one participant. Even though it is a song of himself, it goes beyond himself, and in a subtle, but significant way, shifts the focus from "How **I am the center** of the universe," to "How **I am centered** in the universe." This shift in focus explains the main difference between egoism and self. In egoism, the main story line is all about how "I" can conquer and consume the world around me to satisfy "me, my, mine" needs. In self, the storyline is about the totality of an individual's existence, how what lies within—the world within the individual—responds to the demands made on it by the world that lies outside the individual.

This view of the self is consistent in spirit with the Vedic *"atman"* (the inner invisible self; a part of the eternal, immortal, universal self that exists within each of us). It also aligns with how Carl Jung, one of the three founding giants of psychoanalysis, conceives the self, as the "totality of an individual's conscious and unconscious psyche."

This essay is about self-fueled propulsion of thought and action, because soulful leadership is possible only when leaders can count on themselves, only when they have a lucid and unequivocal sense of self that supports them from within. According to Vedic thought, this competence is achieved only when an individual cultivates and demonstrates three atman-related capabilities.

- *Atman-nirbhar* (self-reliance; no leaning on others, complete reliance on our own inherent capacities to support our emotional and physical wellbeing)

- *Atman-vishwas* (self-belief; complete trust that we can cope with whatever life demands of us in the job called living)

- *Atman-sampurna* (self-sufficiency; zero dependence on external symbols of recognition, reward, praise, prestige to prop us up).

Consequently, even though the essay is titled, "Self-reliance," it's impossible to discuss it completely without also integrating self-belief and self-sufficiency, as the following case-study illustrates.

On the fifth anniversary of the raid on Abbottabad which killed Osama Bin Laden, President Barak Obama relived the decision-making process that led to the final go ahead for the mission in an exclusive interview with CNN's national security analyst, Peter Bergen. The entire interview is riveting, but from this essay's perspective, what's most important is what happened the night of April 28, 2011. With his team of advisors divided on whether or not the risky raid should go ahead, President Obama retired for the night saying he would inform them of his decision in the morning.

The road President Obama traveled that night, he traveled alone. The pros and cons he juggled, he juggled alone. Because after all the votes are in, all hands raised, and all ayes voiced—go, no go—the responsibility of making the decision still remains; the leader still needs to give an unequivocal command. What enabled President Obama to give an unequivocal command the next day was not what he learned at Harvard Law School, or his knowledge of historical precedents, or his reliance on populist platforms. What sustained him and pulled him through, despite his own fears, doubts, and anxieties (and he had plenty of them), was his self-reliance. He took into account the inputs of all his advisors, but made his own call. He understood that significant risks and sacrifices were involved—lives of marines, cost of the mission, USA's international image and reputation, his own image and reputation—yet decided to proceed, because he believed it was in the larger good, in the best interests of his country, USA, and the world's war on terror. He was certain his opponents would scream for his head if the mission failed. But deep within he knew he could rely on himself to cope with the fallout and the brickbats, if it came to that.

Leadership is a humanistic journey. It is natural that team members, humans, will not always see eye-to-eye with the leader. Even leaders may not see eye-to-eye with themselves, as when multiple inner voices peddle them contradictory advice. These differences, disagreements, and contradictions are accentuated during times of crisis, resulting in leaders traveling the proverbial last mile alone in search of unequivocal action. At times like this, only self-reliance can help a leader—not the past (historical precedents), not the present (majority opinion), nor anyone else that the world awards exalted status (experts, consultants, gurus). Not even God, because as the old adage reminds us, "God helps those who help themselves." Or as Caratch, an army general in John Fletcher's play, *Bonduca*, reminds the Queen of England more poetically before the battle against the Romans:

"... The gods love courage arm'd with confidence...
...our valors are our best gods..."

The essential characteristics of soulful leadership, namely the ability to integrate, reconcile, and balance the demands of the moment with the needs of others and oneself, and commit unequivocally to action, all lie within us. Imagination, improvisation, and creative adaptation, indispensable attributes of a soulful leader, come into play only when we release and let go of our misconceptions that authorities external to us have the answers and the power to guide us.

The world's leading scriptures, scholars, philosophers, poets, and artists all agree on this. The Vedic perspective, *atman-nirbhar* (self-reliance), *atman-vishwas* (self-belief), and *atman-sampurna* (self-sufficiency) was shared at the beginning of this chapter. Buddhism advises similarly, "do not seek outside of yourself." As does Christianity, "the kingdom of God lies not 'lo here' not 'lo there'; it lies within." Michelangelo, a peerless genius and creator, believed every block of stone had a statue hidden inside it. It was his job to discover it by believing in himself and his labor. In his timeless essay on Self-Reliance, Emerson advises "Trust thyself: every heart vibrates to that iron string," and declares that, "to believe your own thought...to believe that what is true in your private heart" is what is true genius. Alfred Adler's students, Willard and Marguerite Beecher, say it equally visually in their book, "Beyond Success and Failure: Ways to Self-Reliance and Maturity," when they write, "Human beings are not *empty jugs* waiting to be filled with wisdom by *big jugs*."

Self-reliance is at even a greater premium in times of leadership successions. Particularly when outgoing leaders are tough acts to follow, or when incoming leaders inherit messy environments. In both cases, powerful stakeholder groups could be impossible to please, either due to irrational attachments to the outgoing regime, or because of the impossibility of resolving the inherited mess speedily and making things better for everybody. In their desire to play it safe, incoming leaders may bench self-reliance and defer their personal initiative to external authorities, like tradition and popular opinion. They may even be tempted to mold their thoughts and action to resemble leaders who preceded them, look and talk like them and retell dead tales. But that's a recipe for failure, and the antithesis of soulful leadership. Leadership roles and journeys always unfold in the present, never in the past. Situations change, people change, challenges facing organizations change, policies that succeeded in the past are unlikely to succeed in the future, all of which requires leaders to write fresh histories for their organizations; to create their own footprints through self-reliance, not merely fill others' shoes.

A global leader who has successfully resisted this temptation, and who is a brilliant example of how self-reliance nurtures soulful leadership is Pope Francis, the leader of the Catholic Church. Pope Francis experienced a challenging succession, and inherited a church and religion in denial, turmoil, and disarray. To his credit, he didn't kneel before institutional expectations, capitulate to criticism hurled by experts and the general public, or buckle under the deadweight of tradition. Instead, taking Whitman's cue, he "celebrated himself…invited his soul" and set about playing his role and navigating his leadership journey in a distinctly unique and self-reliant way.

The world acknowledges Pope Francis as being different and recognizes he thinks, says, and behaves as no other Pope before him. It is not just his humble Argentinian origins or his visible departure from ostentation—his plain white cassock, his silver ring, plain metal cross, ordinary black shoes, where he lives, where he eats, or his open Pope mobile. It is his mission to refocus the Catholic church through his resolute self-reliance that has grabbed the world's imagination. Even the most rabid opponents of Catholicism and the Vatican, even atheists, applaud him, and can relate to the merit of his views, words, and actions. Not only has Pope Francis not shied away from tackling sensitive topics confronting the church and society, like divorced Catholics, abortion, climate change, gay marriage, poverty, and the current refugee crisis in Europe, he has actively and fearlessly confronted them. Mainly because he knows that tough issues can't be avoided, but equally importantly because he knows he must travel that road alone—no one else can travel it for him.

If you can keep your head when all about you
Are losing theirs and blaming it on you,
If you can trust yourself when all men doubt you,
But make allowance for their doubting too;
Rudyard Kipling, Lines from "If"

The opening lines of Rudyard Kipling's poem, "If", are impeccably reflected in Pope Francis' behavior. He has kept his head, and he trusts himself and the gospel he preaches. He has also made allowances for others doubting, and confronted vigorously all that afflicts the Catholic Church: power, wealth, status, bigotry, hypocrisy, and above all ego. Only a courageous and self-sufficient person could have exhibited this deep sense of self-reliance.

Another world leader who went through an extremely challenging transition, and who epitomizes self-reliance is Nelson Mandela, South Africa's first black President. It would have been easy, and understandable, for him to have surrendered to the populist demands of black South Africans and other non-white minorities for avenging the cruelty and oppression of apartheid—and his own 27 long years in prison—by resorting to hatred and revenge. But deep within himself, he knew that sacrificing the perpetrators of apartheid would only perpetuate pain and suffering, and it would not win South Africa the new social, economic, and psychological freedoms it needed and wanted. So he opted for peace, reconciliation, and multi-racial co-existence instead, despite extreme and often violent opposition to his views and policies. He was willing to walk alone if necessary, but not sacrifice his "self-reliance," or his commitment to "soulful leadership." The wellbeing and prosperity of the entire country had to increase, which would be impossible if the oppressed became the oppressors.

"Do not judge me by my successes, judge me by how many times I fell down and got back up again," is what Nelson Mandela requested. Only fitting then that we pair this essay with William Henley's poem, "Invictus," a poem that helped Nelson Mandela get back up again…and again…and again…during his 27-years of incarceration, and transformed him as a person and as a leader.

INVICTUS

Out of the night that covers me,
Black as the pit from pole to pole,
I thank whatever gods may be
For my unconquerable soul.

In the fell clutch of circumstance
I have not winced nor cried aloud.
Under the bludgeonings of chance
My head is bloody, but unbowed.

Beyond this place of wrath and tears
Looms but the Horror of the shade,
And yet the menace of the years
Finds and shall find me unafraid.

It matters not how strait the gate,
How charged with punishments the scroll,
I am the master of my fate,
I am the captain of my soul.

William Henley

What makes "Invictus" even more compelling is that William Henley just didn't write a poem that screams self-reliance, he lived and exemplified it. Henley contracted tuberculosis of the bone as a young boy. The disease spread to his foot, and at the age of 25, doctors had to amputate his foot in order to save his life. He wrote this poem while in his hospital bed.

He didn't rail against his circumstance...*I have not winced or cried aloud.* Instead, he turned to his inner strength and willed himself to be *atman-nirbhar...I thank whatever gods there may be for my unconquerable soul.* He didn't despair...*And yet the menace of the years finds and shall find me unafraid.* Because of his unshaken self-reliance, self-belief, and self-sufficiency...*I am the master of my fate, I am the captain of my soul.*

Your turn now, dear reader. What role can you play in growing self-reliance both within yourself and within your organization.

THINK ABOUT IT

- "In the fell clutch of circumstance"—think about circumstances in which you tend to be most self-reliant? Next, think about circumstances that trip you up, where you feel you are less self-reliant than you should be?

TALK ABOUT IT

- How would people who truly believe they are the "master of their fate…captain of their soul" talk and behave in moments of adversity? Role-play an adversity from work, say being overlooked for a promotion. Or, from life outside work, say distress caused by wily friends and family.

ACT ON IT

- Individually, or as a team, adopt some symbolic phrase or behavior that would promote a greater "master of my/our fate…captain of my/our soul" mindset. The world of advertising is a rich source from which to borrow: Nike's signature slogan, "Just do it," oozes self-reliance. Or craft your own, for example, "The flag is still flying," "Down maybe, out never." Your passion for self-reliance will fuel your creativity.

AUTHENTICITY

We are the hollow men
We are the stuffed men...
T.S. Eliot, "The Hollow Men"

There is a reason why we don't pay $10 for a Rolex watch sold on Manhattan's Fifth Avenue. Because the watch is **not what it claims to be**. In short, it is not authentic. The same can be said for leaders. Who they claim to be must match who they are for people to engage with them in a trusting way, and for soulful leadership to manifest itself.

Our histories and experiences advise us that lofty words are easy, but lofty actions to match the loftiness of our words is difficult. Hence the time-honored proverb, "Actions speak louder than words." Alfred Adler, the noted psychoanalyst, had something similar in mind when he said, "Trust only movement" (how people's feet move—what they do—not what they say). This explains why most people are weary of leaders who claim to have our best interests at heart, but don't behave consistent with their claims. Consider the following examples.

During the primaries leading up to the 2016 US Presidential election, Bernie Sanders surprised everybody—network and cable news channels, political pundits, and the average Jack and Jill news junkies—with the support he received from young voters. At one of the Sanders rallies, a TV journalist stopped a young woman and asked her why she preferred Bernie Sanders over Hillary Clinton. This is what she said: "When Bernie speaks, I feel he is speaking his own words, but when Hillary speaks, I feel she is speaking with words someone else has put in her mouth."

The young lady explained authenticity better than any textbook on leadership could have. The perception that a leader is speaking words that someone else has put in her mouth has a *hollow* ring. It makes us wonder where these leaders' allegiances lie, and whether they will actually follow through on their stated commitment to *our* wellbeing and prosperity, or will they sacrifice *us and our interests* in favor of their own. In terms of the theme of this book, we wonder whether these types of leaders are capable of embracing and practicing soulful leadership.

The example that follows is also a real event. Names of the organization and individuals involved have been withheld. At 10 am, in a town hall mentoring meeting, the Senior VP of Client Development at a fast-growing environmental consulting company advises a group of hand-picked high potential executives—next generation leaders—that, "The most important job of a leader is to hire people who think differently and who have the courage to speak their mind." Later that afternoon, while presenting a new strategy for segmenting the market, the same VP displayed intolerance for the virtues he had espoused earlier in the morning: he silenced, rather gruffly, a young next-generation leader (who had attended the morning meeting) who had the courage to think differently and challenge the VP's proposed recommendations by pointing out, "The market has changed, the majority of our customers are buying consulting differently."

In both instances, the divergence between the public and private self of the leader, as reflected by the discrepancy between their claimed intent (words) and exhibited intent (actions) had a grievous effect: it eroded trust, leaving people wondering whether they would truly flourish under the leadership of the person on stage. Inauthentic behaviors, whether words, actions, or both, occur for only one reason, so leaders can use their power and resources to increase their own wellbeing and prosperity. The wellbeing and prosperity of others is relevant only to the extent that it is instrumental to their own, which is the main reason why inauthentic leadership behavior and the adoption and implementation of soulful leadership are not compatible.

Watch your thoughts, they become words
Watch your words, they become actions
Watch your actions, they become habits
Watch your habits, they become character
Watch your character, it becomes your destiny
Introspection from "Eastern Wisdom Cultures"

Before proceeding with aspects of thought, speech, and behavior that cultivate and nurture authenticity and the practice of soulful leadership, it is important to address two challenges to it that could potentially be perceived as undermining this essay's theme. The first perspective, shared even by some leadership gurus, questions the relevance of authenticity. It declares that leaders don't need to be authentic, they merely need to be pragmatic. This essay agrees that leaders need to be pragmatic, but it also declares, politely but vehemently, that authenticity and pragmatism are not incompatible, as the following example illustrates.

The passing of the Civil Rights Bill during Lyndon Johnson's presidency is an excellent example of authenticity and pragmatism co-existing. In 1964, President Lyndon Johnson, an authentic Civil Rights champion, pushed through the Civil Rights Act without voting rights. Not because he had suddenly become unauthentic, but because pragmatism warranted it. He was in danger of losing the entire voting block represented by the southern states, and possibly the election, which would have negated, even reversed, years of progress he had made on the civil rights front. Once elected President Lyndon Johnson, still a committed and authentic Civil Rights champion, resurrected the missing voting rights issue and presided over the passing of the Voting Rights Act in 1965.

A second perspective asserts that authenticity is not always virtuous, or doesn't always lead to positive consequences. This perspective points out that leaders can be authentic *and* have zero interest in being a force of wellbeing and prosperity for the greater many. Totalitarian leaders, monarchs, and other ruthless business leaders are often served up as examples. Such leaders exist even today. Leadership experts and political commentators cite Vladimir Putin as an example. He doesn't pretend to be something other than who he is, and who he is doesn't bode favorably for the wellbeing and prosperity of the many. Worldviews that favor his own wellbeing and prosperity always take precedence in determining who wins and who loses.

This essay agrees that authenticity can play out in different ways. But that perspective actually bolsters the theme of this essay, rather than undermines it. No doubt, forgeries of Picasso and Monet are inauthentic. But the artists who paint them could be authentic, albeit, in a deceiving, self-serving way. They are willing to sacrifice everybody else for their own gain. This type of authenticity is not the focus of this essay, as people and resources are deliberately sacrificed for personal gain. Neither of which reflect an inner awakening, which is non-negotiable for the practice of soulful leadership. The real issue then is how to *increase the supply of authenticity in the service of soulful leadership.* The remainder of this essay will focus on this concern. Three factors are particularly vital in increasing the supply of authenticity in the service of soulful leadership.

First is substance. Authentic leaders are people of substance. Vessels of value, they always have something to offer and are neither "hollow" nor "stuffed," a reference to T.S. Eliot's lines that introduce this essay. Hollow leaders—empty suits—male or female, can rarely be authentic practitioners of soulful leadership. They may say all the right things, but the words rarely get past slogan mongering. Invariably they serve as camouflage, diverting attention away from the leader's inability to take a stand and act unequivocally. Slogans rarely suffice in fueling and sustaining the forward momentum of organizations, which is one of the key jobs of leaders; it is substance that invariably wins the day.

Second is consistency. Authentic leaders are reliable; they have a high degree of internal correlation between how they think, what they say, and how they act. And not just every other Monday, but every single day. They are not bundles of contradictions who confuse, frustrate, and exhaust their organizations by constantly altering their stance, or by demanding that their troops chase the management fashions of the day. That is not to say that once they commit to a certain course of action they stubbornly stick to it, regardless of changing context and consequences. Consistency means there is a continuous and clearly comprehensible rationale that guides leaders' decisions, regardless of whether those decisions concern staying the course, or changing course. For leaders of commercial organizations, it could be a passion or a guiding principle concerning customer service (Ritz-Carlton, Tesco, Flipkart), or product excellence (Bose, Siemens, Sun chef knives). For leaders of organizations from other institutions of society it could be a guiding principle, like non-violence, racial equality, equal educational opportunity, or "truth—the scaffold that sways the future" (the exchange between Martin Luther King, Jr. and a news reporter presented earlier in the essay on "Immortal Poems: New Teachers, New Insights"). Consistency also helps leaders bring clarity and purpose to the implementation of their leadership journeys, since their public selves, their world views and manifestos, are invariably in harmony with the beliefs and convictions that reside in their private selves.

Third is originality, authentic leaders are anything but Xerox copies. They have no desire to pass off as someone else. Just like in the field of men's tennis, Roger Federer, Pete Sampras, Bjorn Borg, and Rod Laver were all great champions, not because they were carbon copies of each other, but because they were originals. They wouldn't have been half as good had they developed their games mimicking and aping other greats. As with leaders: the most effective being those who develop their own unique footprint and signature, a trait that is vital for embracing and serving soulful leadership. They live as the existentialist Albert Camus advises:

"But above all, in order to be, never try to seem."

Two outstanding examples of originality – and authenticity – are Tim Cook, CEO of Apple, and Jeff Immelt, CEO of GE. Both of them would have experienced tremendous pressure "to try to seem" as they assumed their leadership roles, since the persons they followed, Steve Jobs and Jack Welch, had iconic status and gargantuan reputations. For a while, the world believed that "The Jack Welch Way" was the only way to lead a company to greatness. And the same world heralded "The Steve Jobs Way" as *the* way to build and grow a cutting-edge technology company.

But both Tim Cook and Jeff Immelt had the awareness and inner wisdom to recognize that continuing to run Apple and GE as if they were Steve Jobs or Jack Welch would have been unauthentic. They had different skills and capabilities compared to their predecessors, they thought and spoke differently, and most importantly they didn't agree with all the policies, plans, and practices of their predecessors. They had their own ideas on how to take their companies forward. And despite being written off by the media, Wall Street, and many leadership gurus as not being in the same league as their iconic predecessors, despite facing round-the-clock criticism, despite the brouhaha accompanying every percent drop in their stock price, the two stayed the course, put in the hard yards, and led their companies as originals, not as proxies for Steve Jobs and Jack Welch.

Not surprisingly, the same folk who had earlier written them off now celebrate them.

—Rather than being criticized for not being in the same league as Steve Jobs, Tim Cook is now applauded for being in a different league; for his well-managed ego, for his more open, approachable, we-oriented leadership style, for raising the public profile of his executives and for sharing the limelight with them, for championing philanthropy and giving, and for using his privileged platform to confront burning social issues like racial equality and gay rights. All hallmarks of a soulful leader.

—Jeff Immelt too is applauded for many of the same things, but most notably for leading GE his own way, and not Jack Welch's way. He, too, is applauded for his laid-back, informal, people-centric style of leading, for making imagination a growth platform within GE, for embracing the developing world, for actively investing in local manufacturing and R&D facilities around the world, for being courageous to walk away from the past and reimagine GE's future as the world's future premier digital industrial company.

*"All other swindlers upon earth are nothing compared
to self-swindlers."*

Charles Dickens, "Great Expectations"

That's one thing authentic leaders don't do, swindle themselves. Cheating and deceiving oneself is always too high a price to pay. They are awake within to know that swindling themselves will eventually weaken them as leaders and obstruct their leadership journeys.

It is also the essence of Lord Polonius' advice to Laertes in Shakespeare's Hamlet. Three lines perhaps, but the poem is masterly in enabling us to peer into the heart of authenticity. It is timeless in its appeal, because no matter how many times we have read these lines before, each time we read them, they always offer us cause to pause and nudge us to think afresh about its central message—to thine own self be true.

This above all: to thine own self be true,

And it must follow, as the night the day,

Thou canst not then be false to any man.

William Shakespeare, Lines from "Hamlet"

THINK ABOUT IT

- Turn to Camus—"But above all, in order to be, never try to seem." Are there aspects of your own life where the need "to seem," "to become," is interfering with your ability "to be?"

TALK ABOUT IT

- "Not walking the talk" is a leading indicator of the absence of authenticity. Discuss with your peers where it's hurting your work group the most. Brainstorm a few ideas on what can be done to narrow the discrepancy between the walk and talk, if not totally eliminate it.

ACT ON IT

- Based on your reflections and discussions, identify the most important change you would like to see in increasing authenticity in your organization. Then follow Mahatma Gandhi's advice: "You must be the change you wish to see in the world." Launch a community or group to be the change you want to see happen, so others can follow. Someone has to kick it off, may as well be you.

THE LEADER'S WORLD: HOW THE LEADER THINKS...

VISION

"Would you tell me, please, which way I ought to go from here?"
"That depends a good deal on where you want to get to," said the Cat.
"I don't much care where—" said Alice.
Lewis Carroll, "Alice's Adventures in Wonderland"

Unlike Lewis Carroll's Alice, leaders don't have the luxury of not caring where they get to; they are required and paid to care. Or, as the late Dag Hammarskjöld, UN's first secretary general put it, leaders are appointed to their roles, "to - - -" (care where their organizations are headed). Leaders don't have to be visionaries—it helps if they are—but they are expected to have a vision for where they want to take the organizations and people they lead. So, before leaders require their organizations and people to act in decisive and committed ways, they must first formulate decisive and committed answers to two questions. The first, people in their organizations are likely to ask, "*Where* are we headed, Captain?" The second, leaders should ask themselves even if nobody else asks them, "Where *should* we be headed?"

The questions may appear simple, but the process of arriving at answers is complex and challenging. Determining the *where* and the *should* of leadership journeys requires leaders to commit and make choices. It is one of the few aspects of leadership that externalizes what lies within leaders—who they are, what they stand for, and what legacy they want to leave through their leadership journeys. If the leaders are conflicted and muddled within, it will reflect in their vision. Their vested interests and values, whether broadcast to the world or not, will reflect in their vision. How they reconcile and balance their own needs with the needs of others in the ecosystem within which the organization operates will reflect in their vision. Which is what makes vision—how leaders formulate and live it—a vital aspect of soulful leadership. And which is why soulful leaders are advised to work extra hard on its essential elements, the 3Cs—clarity, choice, and commitment.

The first C, clarity of purpose, is crucial because it promotes shared meaning, and coordinated action. By setting boundaries, and pointing at desired horizons, it enables forward momentum, which significantly increases the perceived value of one's work and engagement with the organization. Employees no longer begin their day by thumping their desks, and asking, "What the hell am I doing here?" Or as Piet Hein, the multi-thinker, universalist-humorist puts it:

I'd like to know
what this whole show
is about
before it's out.
Piet Hein, "Grooks"

Most psychotherapists and counsellors regularly admit that beyond a general desire of "I want to be happy...and successful...and make money", most people are extremely foggy about the "what," "where" and "ought to" aspects of their life journeys. Specifying precisely, and concretely what they really want from life, what would truly make them happy, what they regard as success and how much they are willing to sacrifice to get what they want, is often like scaling Everest without oxygen for most people. So they stay with whatever momentum is pushing or pulling them along, even if it's sucking the life out of them. The first part of Newton's law of inertia confirms this—a body at rest stays at rest, and a body in motion stays in motion with the same speed in the same direction. Leaders are no exception. In the name of tradition and staying close to their knitting, they find it easier to continue doing what they have been doing, especially if things are working and the organization is meeting its goals. Even institutional folk lore endorses it, "If it ain't broke, don't fix it." They wake up only when the second part of Newton's law of inertia kicks in, "...unless acted upon by an unbalanced force," meaning when they get whacked on the head and their life journeys run aground.

Which is why "more of the same" is not clarity of purpose. The former represents passive momentum powered by inertia, the latter demands actively generating momentum powered by preferences. Soulful leaders don't take the easy way out and allow mere momentum to dictate their vision: they toil to create momentum. First, by establishing and then clearly communicating the "where" and "ought to" of their leadership journeys.

Let's drop in again on Tim Cook of Apple and Jeff Immelt of GE who we visited in the previous essay, and take a peek at how they have invested in establishing clarity of purpose in their respective companies.

- **Tim Cook:** "We believe that we are on the face of the earth to make great products and that's not changing...We believe in saying no to thousands of projects, so that we can really focus on the few that are truly important and meaningful to us."

- **Jeff Immelt:** "We're a narrower company...and we're a deeper company...we are walking away from financial businesses and playing into this global infrastructure need... playing into those things that the world needs."

Clarity of purpose is not fixed and immutable. It will require fine-tuning and, sometimes, even resetting, as emerging market realities (such as affordable innovation), political developments (such as rise in protectionism), and new technologies (such as wearable technology and Industrial Internet of Things) test soulful leadership by reshaping the landscape of tomorrow's gains and losses. That is why this essay will stay clear of discussing traditional vision and mission statements that adorn the lobbies, websites, and balance sheets of many organizations. Because while they may be elegant symbols of organization identity, they are static and have zero "GPS" value in guiding soulful leadership journeys. Soulful leaders are aware of this. So when the world they operate in changes the rules of the game for determining who wins and who loses, they don't respond symbolically by tinkering with words in vision statements, they respond substantially by resetting the "where" and "ought to" coordinates of their leadership journeys. Currently, Jeff Immelt is in the process of reconfiguring his vision and keeping his soulful leadership journey lively as he guides GE away from the physical world of industrial manufacturing that brought "good things to life," to a digital industrial existence that connects the physical-digital worlds and "makes the world work better."

Two other leaders who this book and others would recognize and acknowledge as soulful leaders merit a visit: Alan Mulally, former CEO of Ford, and Ratan Tata, the executive head of the Tata Group of companies. The clarity with which both of them set the "where" and "ought to" coordinates of their leadership journeys is exemplary, especially as both assumed leadership roles in companies with institutionalized inertia (decades of rich, set-in-concrete histories).

- **Alan Mulally:** "The vision—desire to move, freedom of mobility—will remain constant...our role will evolve... there are tremendous opportunities for safe and efficient transportation in the future...so we might be part of connecting different modes of transportation—bicycles, waterways, cars, buses, subways...all still part of the vision of enabling movement and bringing people together."

- **Ratan Tata:** "We have two guiding arrows...one points overseas, where we want to expand markets for our existing products...the other points right here, to India, where we want to explore the large mass market that is emerging... not by following...but by breaking new ground...doing something that hasn't been done before."

Clarity of purpose is also critical because it directly influences the second C—choice. Leaders are hired to play in sandpits of uncertainty: their No. 1 job is to create better tomorrows. Merely because an organization, institution, or country, is successful today, doesn't mean it'll be successful tomorrow. However, since organizations and their leaders also experience nostalgia, retained memories of yesterday's successes and failures can often chain them to a "business as usual" mindset. How much and what aspects of one's rich and storied past should be remembered, and how much and what aspect of it should be forgotten to make way for new histories poses significant challenges for even the most soulful leaders.

> *"I don't much care where—" said Alice.*
> *"Then it doesn't matter which way you go," said the Cat.*
> *"—so long as I get SOMEWHERE," Alice added as an explanation.*
> *"Oh, you're sure to do that," said the Cat,*
> *"if you only walk long enough."*
> **Lewis Carroll, "Alice's Adventures in Wonderland"**

Leaders can't be blasé about the intended destination of their leadership journeys. "Somewhere" is rarely acceptable; it has to be a *specific* somewhere. Each specific somewhere has its own associated gains and sacrifices. But the two are rarely proportionally, or equitably, distributed. There are scenarios in which those that shed the most blood don't experience the greatest increase in wellbeing and prosperity, while those who benefit the most may only have sacrificed minimally. Context too plays a key role. The overall level and distribution of wellbeing and prosperity in a manufacturing- industrial world is likely to be different than in a digital-industrial world. There may be a class of employees, machine operators for instance, who may not be better off as a result of the transition to a dominantly digital-industrial world, which is why striking a balance between the gains and sacrifices inherent in different choices of destinations is rarely straightforward. As we saw in the cases of dilemmas and quandaries presented in previous essays, there is no right or wrong answer. This is what makes an inner awakening in leaders essential, especially if leaders want to increase the wellbeing and prosperity of those who possess limited resources and options for pursuing their own betterment.

The "where," "should," and "why" of leadership journeys, or alternate visions, will involve tough competing choices and will, therefore, ignite passions and angst. After all, the losses and gains are experienced by living, breathing human beings, not inanimate names in rectangular boxes on organizational charts. Soulful leaders, however, are seldom deterred just because it's impossible to satisfy and please everybody. They don't dither or wait for clearer skies. Nor do they postpone choosing merely because their constituencies don't agree with them, or because they themselves are burdened by doubt. Most importantly, they don't succumb to the temptation of taking refuge in grand gestures and empty words aimed at placating different factions. Because within themselves, they know that placation is never authentic (the previous essay discussed the importance of authenticity). It is at best paralyzed force that may temporarily suppress and suspend dissent, but will eventually block the forward motion of their leadership journeys.

Shape without form, shade without color
paralyzed force, gesture without motion
T.S. Eliot, "The Hollow Men"

Finally, the third C—commitment. Without commitment, there's always tomorrow, and vision is just shadowy wordplay—an empty promise, sound and fury signifying nothing.

To-morrow, and to-morrow, and to-morrow...

...Life's but a walking shadow, a poor player

That struts and frets his hour upon the stage

And then is heard no more...

...sound and fury,

Signifying nothing.

Shakespeare, "Macbeth"

Visions don't materialize overnight. They are journeys that exact their toll over time. Commitment is the signature on the promissory note, indicating a willingness to pay. Without it, well, there would always be tomorrow...and tomorrow...but eventually even tomorrows run out of patience and turn their backs on defaulters.

Imagine for a moment how different history—the tomorrows of the people who lived then—would have been had Abraham Lincoln not been committed to his vision of emancipating American slaves, had Mahatma Gandhi not paid for his vision of winning India's freedom through a commitment to non-violence, had South Africa's FW de Klerk not been committed to his vision of ending apartheid, especially as it involved sacrificing his own position. In each case, the vision of these leaders were gestures without motion, they took shape and color because it was fueled by commitment – a willingness to pay, frequently with life and blood.

There is no better poem to help us reflect on the soulful power of a compelling vision than Martin Luther King, Jr's, "I Have A Dream." It is commonly referred to as a speech, but even a casual reading will testify that *the speech* is suffused with imagery, metaphors, similes, symbolism, and word rhythms (assonance, alliteration), all elements of handsome poetry. So while the text when laid out on a page may have the look of prose, its spirit and sounds are sheer poetry.

Rather than reproduce the entire text, I have excerpted lines from it to capture the essence of Dr. King's vision, then parsed it further to illustrate how ably it embodies the 3Cs—clarity, choice, commitment. I have taken some liberty with the line-breaks to allow us to peer deeper into the soul of Dr. King's words. I have also refrained from adding any commentary on the lines that follow, because some poems don't require analysis and explanation, merely space for quiet reflection.

This is one of those poems.

Essence of Dr. King's Vision

I have a dream that one day on the red hills of Georgia, the sons of former slaves and the sons of former slave owners will be able to sit down together at the table of brotherhood.

I have a dream that my four little children will one day live in a nation where they will not be judged by the color of their skin but by the content of their character.

I have a dream today!

And when this happens... will be able to join hands and sing...

Free at last! Free at last!

Thank God Almighty, we are free at last!

Clarity

In a sense, we've come to our nation's capital to cash a check.

When the architects of our republic wrote the magnificent words of the Constitution and the Declaration of Independence they were signing a promissory note to which every American was to fall heir.

This note was a promise that all men, yes, black men as well as white men, would be guaranteed the "unalienable Rights" of "Life, Liberty and the pursuit of Happiness."

And so, we've come to cash this check, a check that will give us upon demand the riches of freedom and the security of justice.

Choice

*But there is something that I must say to my people,
who stand on the warm threshold which leads into the
palace of justice: In the process of gaining our rightful
place, we must not be guilty of wrongful deeds.*

*Let us not seek to satisfy our thirst for freedom by
drinking from the cup of bitterness and hatred. We
must forever conduct our struggle on the high plane of
dignity and discipline.*

*We must not allow our creative protest to degenerate
into physical violence. Again, and again, we must rise
to the majestic heights of meeting physical force with
soul force.*

Commitment

*And as we walk, we must make the pledge that we
shall always march ahead.*

We cannot turn back.

*There are those who are asking the devotees of civil
rights, "When will you be satisfied?" We can never be
satisfied as long as the Negro is the victim of the un-
speakable horrors of police brutality.*

*No, no, we are not satisfied, and we will not be satis-
fied until "justice rolls down like waters, and righteousness like a mighty stream."*

THINK ABOUT IT

- What is your vision for your life? Does it have the appropriate amount of clarity, choice, and commitment? Where can you do better?

TALK ABOUT IT

- What forums could exist (and should exist) to encourage people to discuss their dreams and vision for themselves, for the department, and for the company?

ACT ON IT

- Identify at least one obstacle to your personal dream or vision. Then, implement a single initiative tomorrow, or at least within a week, to overcome that obstacle.

Substance

There were...

...a million stars, a million miles, a million people,

a million words, a million places and a million years...

We knew a lot of things we could hardly understand.

Kenneth Fearing, "Collective Poems"

Will Rogers, the famous humorist, once quipped, "Everybody is ignorant, only on different subjects." This is even more true in today's VUCA world (Volatile, Uncertain, Complex, Ambiguous), in which challenges posed by work and the workplace are far too varied and complex for one person to tackle—or even a group of people—no matter how brilliant or heroic. Regardless, leaders are expected to be people of substance. Their organizations expect them to have solutions, or at least intelligent, highly informed points-of-view, for even the most intractable problems.

So how do soulful leaders address this paradox? It's a predicament: leaders must act "substantially," while never really having the luxury of knowing everything to be foolproof, and coping with the unwavering demands of having to virtually guarantee an increase in the future wellbeing and prosperity of their people and organizations. They do so by continuously investing in themselves to learn more, know more, understand more, so they can be more substantial—*without* succumbing to the seductive belief that they know it all. Consequently, soulful leaders feel very comfortable saying, "I don't know" and "I don't understand."

But they don't stop there. They follow up "I don't know" and "I don't understand" with "I am willing to learn," "I am willing to understand." And this is not just posturing. They are acutely aware that a sense of misguided exceptionalism—overvaluing what they know, discounting what they don't know—can be downright dangerous. They are also acutely aware of the dangers of dismissing the power of circumstances and constraints, because they are aware that "what they don't know" can hurt them. Regardless of the merit and power of their intent, they know that even the most brilliant strategies have their nemeses in waiting. Or, as Thomas Hardy suggested in a poem he composed after the disaster—every Titanic has a "sinister mate," an iceberg waiting.

And as the smart ship grew

In stature, grace, and hue,

In shadowy silent distance grew the Iceberg too...

...No mortal eye could see

The intimate welding of their later history

Thomas Hardy, "The Convergence of the Twain."

Keen on avoiding icebergs, soulful leaders throw open the doors of their mind and invest in continuous learning, knowing, and understanding, so that they give themselves the best chance of becoming people of substance.

A little learning is a dangerous thing;
Drink deep, or taste not the Pierian spring:
There shallow draughts intoxicate the brain,
And drinking largely sobers us again.
Fired at first sight with what the Muse imparts,
In fearless youth we tempt the heights of Arts;
While from the bounded level of our mind
Short views we take, nor see the lengths behind,
But, more advanced, behold with strange surprise
New distant scenes of endless science rise!
Alexander Pope, "A Little Learning"

The first part of Alexander Pope's poem, "A Little Learning," presented above, speaks of the dangers of a little learning, and urges us to pursue deep learning. A little learning (*shallow draughts*) befuddles more than it enlightens (*intoxicate the brain*). It can be a dangerous thing because it may seduce and mislead us into thinking we know more than, in fact, we do. Pope doesn't merely point out a problem, he also suggests a remedy. He advises us to go deeper (*drink deep, or taste not the Pierian spring*) because the more we learn, the more we are reminded of how much more there is to learn (*drinking largely sobers us again*), and because deep learning reveals and makes accessible new vistas and possibilities previously denied to us (*New distant scenes of endless science rise!*).

The "Pierian spring" Pope refers to in his poem flows from Greek mythology. Located in Macedonia, it was the sacred place of the Muses and served as a source of inspiration and knowledge of art and science. But that was back then. What are today's Pierian springs? From what sources can today's leaders drink deeply, so they can escape the shallow draughts of little learning and make wiser, more enlightened decisions for the future of the organizations they lead and their own futures?

Soulful leaders drink deeply from four sources to acquire deeper learning and understanding.

First is **transcending blame**. Soulful leaders approach their organizations and work with a growth and learning mindset. They are constantly looking for ways to improve and do better. It's not about finger pointing and apportioning blame, "Who goofed, who screwed up?". It's going beyond that; it's about "Let's figure out a way to do better next time"—because true solutions appear only when leaders are able to travel to places beyond right and wrong, as Rumi so eloquently advises in his brief poem.

Out beyond ideas of wrongdoing and rightdoing,
there is a field. I'll meet you there.
Rumi

When Alan Mulally took over as CEO of Ford, it was not un-common for supervisors to jump all over employees, and launch fault-finding missions, if employees decided to stop production on a vehicle for some reason: "What are you doing? How did this happen?". Mulally worked hard during his tenure to change that to "What can we do to help you out?" — a more productive and helpful way to keep the organization moving forward, and a per-fect reflection of the spirit of Rumi's words and growth-learning mindset.

Next is **asking questions**. In our frantic search for solutions, we sometimes forget there is no better way of learning, under-standing, and establishing a new sense of purpose and direction than ensuring we are asking the right questions.

"The person who asks a question
is ignorant for a few moments,
the person who doesn't
remains ignorant for life."
Confucius

And not just run-of-the-mill questions that rehash and repackage the what is already known, but tough, courageous questions that are typically avoided, or not asked, concerning future possibilities and potentialities—the "what-if?", "why-not?", "what might be a better way?" types of questions. Commonly called strategic questions, they don't merely repackage what is already known, but encourage instead an exploration of previously-considered options regarding change and progress. This is especially helpful when dissent and disagreements abound, and organizations find themselves chasing their tails.

The current pope, Pope Francis, is hailed as the great reformer by his biographer, Austen Ivereigh, largely on account of his ability to challenge convention by asking tough, never-before-asked questions—questions which may not sit well with everybody, but have helped the Catholic Church regain forward momentum by establishing a new sense of purpose. In his book, "Who Says Elephants Can't Dance?" Lou Gerstner, IBM's former CEO, attributes IBM's large-scale transformation and turnaround from the brink of bankruptcy to this very ability: first asking tough questions, then living out the answers to those tough questions, no matter how uncomfortable.

The ability to ask strategic questions is an essential component of a soulful leader's arsenal, because *living the question* is a large part of finding the answer.

"Be patient toward all that is unsolved in your heart and try to love the questions themselves, like locked rooms and like books that are now written in a very foreign tongue...Live the questions now. Perhaps you will then gradually, without noticing it, live along some distant day into the answer."

Rainer Maria Rilke, "Letters To A Young Poet"

The third Pierian spring is **listening**, and its sibling, **observing**. The world, both within the organization and the one in which it operates, presents itself differently when leaders truly listen and observe—hear and see with the ears and eyes of the heart—with empathy. In his famous novel, *Siddhartha,* Herman Hesse shows how everything, even the natural world, sounds different and holds greater wisdom when one truly listens.

"Siddhartha listened...completely absorbed, quite empty, taking in everything...he had often heard all this before, all the numerous voices in the river, but today they sounded different."
Herman Hesse, "Siddhartha"

The importance of listening will also be discussed in a subsequent essay. For the moment, it is sufficient to point out that deep learning and understanding is impossible without deep listening. It's impossible for anyone, leaders included, to truly learn and understand anything worthwhile if they go through life in a "Let me tell you" mode.

Soulful leaders are aware that even though they are often referred to as directors (theater, cinema) and orchestra conductors, they are not just directors and conductors. They are also actors in the play or the movie they are directing, they are also musicians in the orchestra they are conducting, making it vital for them to see and hear what others are saying, doing, or playing, so they can effectively contribute to the overall sum of wellbeing and prosperity created by their leadership journeys.

Finally, soulful leaders invest in their own learning and understanding by **widening their circle of teachers**. They know that learning and understanding often come from the most unexpected sources. Medicine can be informed by art, science by humanities, and organizational psychology by the world of ants, bees, and geese. Business, this book argues, can be informed by poetry. The world is full of teachers; who we learn from is our choice.

William Wordsworth widened his circle of teachers to include nature, and learned a great deal in the process about his own humanity and his relationship with others and this world. Precisely what we need from current and future leaders.

Books! 'tis a dull and endless strife:
Come, hear the woodland linnet,
How sweet his music! on my life,
There's more of wisdom in it...

Come forth into the light of things,
Let Nature be your teacher...

Our meddling intellect
Mis-shapes the beauteous forms of things:–
We murder to dissect.

Enough of Science and of Art;
Close up those barren leaves;
Come forth, and bring with you a heart
That watches and receives.

William Wordsworth (Lines from, "The Tables Turned")

Uncertainty is an inescapable aspect of life. Leaders experience disproportionately more uncertainty because of their roles and the size of the stages on which they perform. Paradoxically though, the organizations they lead expect them to be certain that their leadership journeys will result in greater wellbeing and prosperity. Soulful leaders have an inner awakening to know that the best way to resolve this paradox is by an unwavering commitment to being a person of substance. This involves investing in continuous learning and understanding, and openly accepting and embracing ignorance—the knowledge that no matter how hard they try, there will always be aspects of their organizations they "don't know," and can't "understand."

Just like immortal poems rarely appease us with quick-fix answers to allay our anxieties and uncertainties, soulful leaders, people of substance, rarely attempt to satisfy their organization's hunger for wellbeing and prosperity with quick-fixes and easy solutions. They have an acute inner awareness that, no matter how seductive, quick fixes and easy solutions can only produce false panaceas—never enduring wellbeing and prosperity.

THINK ABOUT IT

- Think about what you can do to convert an honest "I don't know" from a possible liability to an asset. Are you supportive or critical of yourself and others when you run into an honest *I don't know*? For example, think about what makes you reluctant to say, "I don't know." If it's fear of censure or ridicule, think about what you can do to reduce it. Next, look in the rear view mirror and think of how you have reacted when someone else (either senior or junior to you) has said, "I don't know."

TALK ABOUT IT

- Discuss to what extent "manufactured impatience"—the irrational desire to have every problem resolved yesterday—is a roadblock to deeper learning and substance in your team or immediate work group?

ACT ON IT

- The courage to ask questions is one of the strongest indicators of a commitment to learning, knowledge, and understanding. Act on this insight by adopting an, "I don't know," "I'd like to learn" mindset. Simultaneously, encourage others to adopt this mindset as well, by answering their questions patiently and politely. It will give them the permission and freedom to ask even tougher questions in the future.

DOUBT

No doubt about it,
the mountain cuckoo
is a crybaby.
Kobayashi Issa

Is doubt always a weakness in leaders, or can it also be a virtue? The answer depends entirely on how one interprets the question and the word "doubt." If the interpretation focuses on doubting oneself, the absence of self-belief or self-confidence, then virtually everyone would consider that kind of doubt a weakness.

Our doubts are traitors,
and make us lose the good we oft might win,
by fearing to attempt.
Shakespeare, "Measure for Measure"

Thinker-doers, entrepreneurs, and achievers in all fields of life would agree with Shakespeare and label doubt a weakness, if interpreted in this way. After all, they wouldn't have plunged head first into whatever the world recognizes and applauds them for, or kept going even in the face of insurmountable odds, if they had doubted themselves.

Doubt may also be considered a weakness if interpreted as an absence of faith (usually in a divine power). Priests and politicians are forever urging their flock and constituencies to keep the faith. Faith moves mountains, it adds to an individual's power to cope and act, they advise. Correspondingly, doubt diminishes the power of individuals to act and cope.

William Blake condemns this kind of doubt when he says:

He who shall teach the Child to Doubt
The rotting Grave shall ne'er get out...
He who replies to words of doubt
doth put the light of knowledge out...
William Blake, "Auguries of Innocence"

But several philosophers and thinkers, like educator-theologian Paul Tillich, author Kurt Vonnegut, and philosopher Renee Descartes (one of the pioneers of modern Western philosophy, whose entire philosophical adventure began with an act of doubt) disagree with Blake. They advocate and uphold faith, but vigorously advise against the perils of blind faith because they consider doubt and faith as allies, working toward a common goal, namely the search for truth.

"If you would be a real seeker after truth, it is necessary that at least once in your life doubt, as far as possible, all things."

Renee Descartes

While the jobs of leaders are often less lofty than the pursuit of truth, this essay sides with thinkers, like Descartes, who consider doubt and doubting as healthy and, consequently, encourage it for the following reasons.

First, doubt helps keep leaders grounded and keeps expectations and estimates of future success realistic and in-check. Blind faith in numbers and information, no matter how meticulously culled, is rarely an asset. Markets and customers, which are key determinants of the future wellbeing and prosperity of most organizations, are unpredictable and capricious, even in the best of times. In such an environment, leaders who are "overconfident" of their own assessment of outcomes—how the company's new products will wow customers, how emerging competitive threats will fizzle and fade, and how the company's new technologies will drive the company to market leadership—can cause more harm than good.

It's one thing for the poet Kobayashi Issa, whose job is to see and hear things others don't, to have no doubt that the "mountain cuckoo is a crybaby," as noted in his poem above. It's quite another thing if Issa san were the Chief Technology Officer (CTO) of Shopping Cart (hypothetical name) launching a new e-commerce platform for the company, to declare before the company's CEO and executive committee, "No doubt, the new e-commerce platform will increase sales by 25%." Clearly, the CEO and members of the executive committee will be better off doubting Issa san, and asking a boatload of questions to understand what makes the CTO so "cocksure."

Doubt also helps soulful leaders sort through conflicting interests and biased agendas that could potentially wreck the benefits generated by their leadership journeys. Most companies operate in silos. It is quite common for these silos—different departments and functions—to view markets and customers through the prism of their own vested interests, leading to lop-sided evaluations of the attractiveness of future decisions. Consequently, it's in the best interest of leaders to embrace doubt and doubting, so they can get a fuller picture of the likely consequences of their decisions.

Back to Isaa san, the CTO (not the poet), who had "no doubt" concerning the in-market success of the new e-commerce platform. His estimate of a 25% increase in revenue may be built on one narrow aspect of reality, namely, "speed"—the ability of the new platform to handle high-volume transactions quicker. While it certainly brings the advantage of the new technology into focus, it leaves out several other variables, most notably customers, who are not even in the picture. Do all customers have a need for high-volume transactions? Will the benefits of switching to the new platform outweigh the costs associated with the switch for the customer segment that engages in high-volume transactions? Using the doubt card will enable Shopping Cart's CEO to ask relevant questions like, "Who benefits?", "Why now?", "I know the upside, but what's the downside if we don't pursue it?". Or, put another way, doubt and doubting will enable the CEO to develop a comprehensive understanding of the pattern of gains and sacrifices inherent in the decision – "who wins, who loses, who benefits, and who pays?" – which is essential for soulful leadership.

Next, doubt enables preparedness. Leadership journeys, as the previous essay explained, are fraught with uncertainty. And the best-laid plans are often waylaid by "accidents", as Robert Burns apologetically explains to a mouse whose nest he accidentally destroyed while tilling a field.

The best laid schemes o' Mice an' Men (best laid plans...)
Gang aft agley, (often go awry)
An' lea'e us nought but grief an' pain, (and leave us nothing...)
For promis'd joy! (instead of the joy promised).
Robert Burns, Lines from, "To A Mouse"

President Obama's decision to sanction the special operations raid on Abbottabad that killed Osama bin Laden was characterized by both faith and doubt. (This case study was also used in the essay on Self-reliance.) He had faith in the abilities of Admiral William McRaven to lead the mission, and in the skills of the special forces to pull it off. But he—and others on his team—also had doubts. What if the intelligence was flawed? What if Osama bin Laden was not the man in the compound? What if the Pakistanis got wind of the mission and intervened before the special forces could accomplish their mission? What if the events of the failed Iran hostage rescue mission repeated themselves?

The doubting was neither discredited, nor dismissed. Consequently, Admiral McRaven developed several back-up plans to bring the Navy SEALS back safely should things go wrong. And wisely so—things did go wrong. One of the helicopters used in the raid lost lift, descended very quickly, and crashed. But that didn't impair the mission. Back-up plans were deployed, and the SEALS returned safely to base after successfully completing their mission. All because giving credence to doubt had led to a higher level of preparedness.

Doubt and doubting also helps leaders find an effective medium between *stability* and *novelty*. All organizations are constantly juggling two fundamental goals, *stability*— the ability to survive and grow in familiar ways, by preserving past wisdom, and *novelty*—the ability to survive and grow by remaining open to change (adaptation, improvisation, innovation). Caught between these two goals, and never armed with perfect information, leaders are constantly asking themselves, "Knowing what we know now, should we act differently than we have in the past?" If leaders act in ways they always have in the past, they risk the survival of their organizations by failing to pursue more promising futures. Erasing all memory of the past and starting from scratch is not a good option either, as the Spanish pragmatist George Santayana cautions, "Those who cannot remember the past are condemned to repeat it."

"Doubt is an uncomfortable condition,
but certainty is a ridiculous one."
Voltaire

Even though doubt is an uncomfortable condition, soulful leaders pursue future wellbeing and prosperity by doubting the infallibility of yesterday's wisdom, and doubting the guaranteed lucrativeness of tomorrow's failsafe bets. It is the surest way to balance the contradictory demands of stability and novelty, neither of which soulful leaders can ignore.

Finally, doubt is the most powerful antidote to hubris— arrogance bred by success—which, rather than increasing the wellbeing and prosperity of people operating in the system, seriously damages it. It is human nature to attribute success to one's own brilliance, things that leaders and the organization are doing right, and which "no doubt" they can continue doing in the future. That is the biggest fallacy. Soulful leaders know that in addition to their own innate skills and competencies, luck, happenstance, and fortuitous accidents also have a role to play in their success. Consequently, while they take credit, they also leave the door open for doubt, because deep within they know success also carries within it the seeds of failure. Companies like Kodak, Motorola, IBM, and General Motors had "no doubt" of the invincibility of their success formulas, and they suffered irreversible performance setbacks as a result. They were justified in taking credit for their historical success, but not in letting that back-slapping morph into hubris. Once they crossed the threshold and entered the realm of "no doubt," they effectively became blind and deaf to all customer and market signals suggesting that, perhaps, the company was headed in a wrong direction.

"Wrong direction?" "Impossible."

For leaders who don't value, and hence don't encourage doubt, all things that challenge their smug beliefs concerning the rightness of their strategies are impossible. But impossible things do happen. Helicopters built with state-of-the-art technology lose lift and crash. Batteries of the Galaxy Note 7, a next-generation smartphone designed to propel Samsung to market leadership, suddenly begin exploding, resulting in the phone being killed and the company suffering a close to $3 billion loss. The digital world—devices and always-on screens—becomes a stronger source of addiction than drugs. In such a world where prevailing wisdom and "no doubt" points-of-view are frequently dethroned and exiled, it is prudent to cozy up to doubt and doubting. It offers leadership journeys greater insurance as they navigate turbulent and uncertain environments.

Robert Graves' poem, "In Broken Images," is a contrarian poem, and hence tailor-made for pairing with doubt. This essay began by asking a simple question, "Is doubt a weakness, or a virtue?" Let's hear what Robert Graves has to say.

> *He is quick, thinking in clear images;*
> *I am slow, thinking in broken images.*
> *He becomes dull, trusting to his clear images;*
> *I become sharp, mistrusting my broken images,*
> *Trusting his images, he assumes their relevance;*
> *Mistrusting my images, I question their relevance.*
> *Assuming their relevance, he assumes the fact,*
> *Questioning their relevance, I question the fact.*
> *When the fact fails him, he questions his senses;*
> *When the fact fails me, I approve my senses.*
> *He continues quick and dull in his clear images;*
> *I continue slow and sharp in my broken images.*
> *He in a new confusion of his understanding;*
> *I in a new understanding of my confusion*
> **Robert Graves, "In Broken Images"**

Leaders who never suffer from any doubt, who are never ever confused, are rare. Yet, leaders often go to great lengths to portray a persona to the contrary, a "cocksure" person who seldom has doubts. Mainly because that's what the organizations and people they lead expect from them. After all, isn't the job of leaders to dispel confusion? Perhaps. But the more important question is, "How should leaders dispel confusion and bring about the certainty their organizations and the people they lead yearn for?"

According to this essay, they should do it by encouraging and nurturing doubt, not by flaunting an "overconfident" mindset. As Robert Graves explains, through the poem's emphasis on questioning and examining, the act of doubting cultivates clarity and understanding; it makes issues less foggy. Consequently, leaders who actively embrace doubt, who are unafraid to admit experiencing it, and who are comfortable living through their confusion, fill their organizations with a credible certainty, which in turn evokes trust and commitment. Besides, the additional questioning, reflection, and search for understanding that accompanies doubt and doubting gives leaders a chance to make visible, and examine consciously, the pattern of sacrifices—who wins, who loses—inherent in the decisions and choices that characterize their leadership journeys. It is these aspects and properties that make doubt a virtue and a crucial indicator of the presence of soulful leadership.

THINK ABOUT IT

- Both doubting too much and being overly sure make a person vulnerable, and are therefore liabilities. The former cripples action by overemphasizing threats, the latter excessively hastens action by underemphasizing threats. Where do you lie on that continuum?

TALK ABOUT IT

- How are people who like to slow things down so they can "arrive at a new understanding of their confusion" treated by the rest of the organization? Are they respected, or silently (or openly) ridiculed? How they are treated will send a strong signal of whether doubt is an asset or a liability.

ACT ON IT

- Make poetry work for you. Start meetings by reading Robert Graves's poem, "In Broken Images." I have. It works. The poem holds a mirror to us, forcing us to reexamine our reasons for certitude, and encourages us to become "slower and sharper," or at least experiment with Robert Graves' advice.

THE LEADER'S WORLD: HOW THE LEADER ACTS…

RISK

"Come to the edge," he said. "We can't, we're afraid!" they responded.
"Come to the edge," he said. "We can't, we will fall!" they responded.
"Come to the edge," he said.
And so they came. And he pushed them. And they flew.

Christopher Logue

Few forces are as potent as the fear of failure, and the accompanying ridicule, in preventing people from venturing, taking the first several steps so vital for launching life's journeys. Leaders are no exception. In Apollinaire's poem above we get the impression that it is a leader asking *them* (people in the organization) to come to the edge and jump. But it could be the other way around too. *Them* urging leaders to come to the edge. Frequently, we hear people in organizations attribute the slow pace of progress to risk-averse leadership. After all, leaders have more to lose and may favor playing it safe. But leaders and leadership are not about playing it safe.

*"A ship is always safe at the shore...but that is NOT
what it is built for."*
Albert Einstein

Like ships, leaders are expected to sail and, like pilots, they are
expected to navigate leadership journeys to ensure the survival and
growth of their organizations. Risk is interwoven in every phase
of these leadership roles and journeys, because leaving one shore
for another requires trading certainty for uncertainty. Perhaps this
is the reason why so much discussion concerning risk approaches it as if it were a problem, a negative and dangerous thing. But
that's not what we were taught when we're young. The proverb we
heard growing up was, "Nothing ventured, nothing gained." Yes,
there is uncertainty, but there is also gain, a reward for venturing.
Soulful leaders never lose sight of this simple fact. They don't stall
their leadership journeys by obsessing over obstacles and focusing
on risks alone, and they don't blindly turbocharge their journeys by
blindly pursuing rewards. Soulful leaders work hard at embracing
and balancing risk and rewards—figuring out how much risk to
take and when—so they can offer lucid reasons to their organizations for coming to the edge and leaping. The following brief
discussion lays out the skills and resources that soulful leaders rely
upon to persuade their organizations to come to the edge and leap.

The pre-requisite resource is courage.

*"Don't be too timid and squeamish about your actions. All life is an
experiment. The more experiments you make the better."*
Ralph Waldo Emerson

Soulful leaders are neither timid nor squeamish. All leadership journeys, regardless of their destination, are soaked in courage —whether they are a fight against injustice (slavery, colonial oppression, voting rights, apartheid), whether they are journeys in search of new corporate identities (Hallmark, IBM, Samsung, Bidvest, Mitsubishi, Siemens, Reliance industries), or whether they are moonshots to create markets where none existed before, as thousands of entrepreneurs do daily in various Silicon Valleys around the world.

But, their courage is tempered with caution. Soulful leaders confront risk intelligently, and rarely equate it with recklessness.

...If you can make one heap of all your winnings
And risk it on one turn of pitch-and-toss,
And lose, and start again at your beginnings
And never breathe a word about your loss...
Rudyard Kipling, "If"

Risking one's all on a pitch-and-toss and still having the steel to soldier on is the ultimate in inspiration for coping with adversity. However, despite its heroic and romantic appeal, the sentiment that Kipling expresses should be embraced cautiously, because it really carries two messages in one. Soulful leaders don't gamble the future of their organizations; they are not foolish. They have read the histories of companies like Kingfisher Airlines, MCI, and Enron, and know that flamboyant, high-flying leaders may dazzle the world and investors briefly, but ultimately wreck the wellbeing and prosperity of their people and organizations. They are acutely aware that risk can't be intimidated, so they don't even try. Instead, they attempt to tame it and make it an ally through disciplined and courageous experimentation. But if they do take intelligent risks and fall, they get up, rebuild, and move on. Exactly as Kipling advises.

But is that enough? Is it enough for just the leaders to have the courage to risk failure? What about the rest of the organization? Is it not important for the people and the organization to be just as courageous, be willing to risk failure, and not be stopped by it? It is, but *how* they do it is the critical consideration.

"The way to succeed is to double your error rate," is how Thomas J. Watson, former IBM CEO used to rally his company. Watson wasn't the first leader to exhort his company to embrace failure, and he certainly won't be the last one. Every day, numerous leaders around the world exhort their organizations to fail more often and fail better.

Ever tried. Ever failed. No matter.

Try again. Fail again. Fail better.

Samuel Beckett, "Worstward Ho"

However, "failing better" is easier said than done, because standing in the shadow of that error or failure is a person. And people don't like failing, they prefer succeeding. Organizations don't like failing either. More importantly, notwithstanding the "double your error rate" or "fail better" rhetoric, rewards and recognition in most organizations are usually showered on people who succeed, not those who fail. How then can leaders encourage their people to maintain a positive and proactive attitude toward risk-taking? Especially if the people know or believe that failing can damage their career, and in some cases even cost them their job?

There is only one real way, by building courageous organizational cultures that are truly tolerant of failure and encourage risk-taking by treating failure as a genuine opportunity for learning.

If you can meet with Triumph and Disaster
And treat those two impostors just the same
Rudyard Kipling, "If"

Anything less would send confused signals and inhibit risk taking, potentially depriving the organization and its people of potentially greater wellbeing and prosperity in the future. Are there enough of these courageous cultures on view? Perhaps not, which makes the need for soulful leadership even more urgent.

Finally, in addition to cultivating courage in themselves and investing in building courageous cultures, soulful leaders tame risk and make it work for them by remaining *open* to new ideas and suggestions. They are acutely aware that risk does not yield to rank or authority, because seniority alone doesn't guarantee a ringside seat to the full range of possibilities, especially in times of crises. So in order to establish a more effective working equation with risk, soulful leaders cast a wide net and engage in collaboration.

The 2010 Chilean mining disaster illustrates vividly all three elements—leader's courage, courageous culture, and collaboration—that characterize how soulful leaders approach and negotiate risk to keep their leadership journeys moving forward. The challenge following the collapse of the mine was to safely and quickly drill a hole through hundreds of feet of rock and rescue the trapped miners. Several drilling options, each with their own risk-reward profile, were considered, and although six separate drilling efforts were implemented within a week of the accident, the leadership team led by André Sougarret **doubted** whether any of them would succeed in drilling fast enough to the shelter in which the miners were trapped. This doubting made Andre Sougarret open and receptive to drilling alternatives, and listening to others' ideas.

Consequently, when 24-yearold field engineer Igor Proestakis, an employee of Drillers Supply, SA not involved with the official rescue effort, arrived at the accident scene on his own with an idea, he found in Señor Sougarret a willing listener. Igor Proestakis' idea was to use an American company's (Core Rock) cluster hammer technology because he believed it could cut through the hard rock a lot quicker than the competing technologies deployed. That sounded extremely promising to Sourraget, for whom the safety and rescue of the miners was paramount. But that *benefit* was not without *risk*. Proestakis had two strikes against him: his age and his lack of experience. After cautiously weighing the risks and benefits, Sourraget decided to give Proestakis a chance—a decision that proved prescient because, exactly as he had explained, Proestakis and his team were the first to drill through to the miners.

The case is an excellent example of soulful leadership in action, and carries numerous learnings for how leaders can (and should) engage with risk. Every leadership decision involves risk (the reality of the unknown, the unpredictability of outcomes) and fear (fear of the unknown and of failure). Since fear amplifies the perception of risk, it often breeds inaction by delaying and derailing the timing of executive decisions, which ironically increases risk. Soulful leaders are aware of this, so they don't *risk inaction*, neither do they throw caution to the winds and *risk reckless action*. Sourraget had no way of being sure which technology would help him meet his goal of rescuing miners safely and in the quickest time possible. But he didn't let that delay the implementation of the rescue mission. To combat and contain the risk, he *experimented*, carefully evaluated alternatives, and implemented several drilling technologies concurrently. At the same time, he actively doubted whether any of the options that he and his team had implemented would help them achieve their goal. Rather than convincing him to retreat, this doubting opened him up to possibilities. It made him even more willing to travel further from home, listen, collaborate, and take even more risk. Proestakis could have been sent packing on several counts—he showed up uninvited, he was young, and he lacked experience. But, if Proetakis came through, it was only partially due to his own initiative and ingenuity. It was also due in large measure because a soulful leader was willing to listen and risk giving him a chance. Paradoxically, the risk Sourraget took by engaging and collaborating with Proestakis actually lowered the overall risk of the rescue mission, and increased the chances of the mission achieving its goal in a speedy, yet safe way. In summary, Sourraget didn't just stick with the tried and tested and familiar, and doubt the unknown, instead he doubted what he knew and embraced what he should have doubted, the new and unfamiliar. Of course, he did so cautiously and intelligently, after carefully considering the risks and rewards, which gave him and his team the courage to come to the edge and leap.

Some poems are immortal because they live on in our hearts and minds long after we've read them, often on the strength of a single word (Rudyard Kipling's "If"), or a single line. Robert Frost's poem, "The Road Not Taken," is such a poem. It nests in millions of minds and hearts around the world through one dominant line, "Two roads in the woods I met...." Never mind that the millions recall the line differently than how Frost wrote it, "Two roads diverged in a yellow wood...." Never mind that they recall the title differently, confusing it with M. Scott Peck's book, "The Road Less Traveled." Never mind that they don't associate the poem with Frost, or remember any other words and lines from the poem; never mind all that. Each time these millions stand at a crossroad and confront a difficult—and hence risky—choice, Frost's signature line arises in their consciousness, and they stop and think and ask themselves, "Which road should I take?" Which is what makes Frost's poem, "The Road Not Taken," an ideal teacher for educating soulful leaders on the importance and role of "risking" in their leadership journeys, without being "reckless."

Two roads diverged in a yellow wood,
And sorry I could not travel both
And be one traveler, long I stood
And looked down one as far as I could
To where it bent in the undergrowth;

Then took the other, as just as fair,
And having perhaps the better claim,
Because it was grassy and wanted wear;
Though as for that the passing there
Had worn them really about the same,

And both that morning equally lay
In leaves no step had trodden black.
Oh, I kept the first for another day!
Yet knowing how way leads on to way,
I doubted if I should ever come back.

I shall be telling this with a sigh
Somewhere ages and ages hence:
Two roads diverged in a wood, and I—
I took the one less traveled by,
And that has made all the difference.

Robert Frost, "The Road Not Taken"

Undoubtedly, "Two roads diverged in a yellow wood…" is a line for the ages. But, the two lines of the penultimate stanza are just as compelling.

> *Yet knowing how way leads on to way,*
> *I doubted if I should ever come back.*

Yes, just as way does lead on to way, decisions lead on to other decisions, opening some doors, closing others. The consequences of decisions—including not making a decision—are often irreversible, which makes the influence of an inner awakening in leaders even more important in confronting and negotiating risk intelligently.

Yet sometimes, despite their best intentions to confront risk intelligently, despite their best efforts to seek extra information and collaboration, soulful leaders may find the roads that diverge in the "yellow wood" of everyday life and circumstances still unclear and foggy.

Which way—left or right? Should we, shouldn't we?

What then? What do leaders do when they are all knotted and tangled, where do they go? As an earlier essay advised us, there is only one place they can (and should) go for advice after they've checked off all the boxes and paid homage to every rule in their own rule book—they should go deep within. There is only one person and source they can (and should) trust when risking a fork in the road—their own self and humanity (*atman nirbhar and ataman sampurna*; self-reliant and self-confident).

Above all, leaders should consider doing the one thing they were hired to do. Act. Go to the edge, and leap. It is what leadership demands, and how soulful leaders respond.

THINK ABOUT IT

- Are there times in your life when you missed opportunities for personal growth and prosperity because you stayed ashore? When you were afraid to disagree, or make a contrary suggestion? Conversely, are there times in your life when you suffered because you leapt, or set sail, without "doubting" enough the rosy outcomes you wished and hoped would materialize? What can you do to improve your abilities to take intelligent risks? The answers lie within you.

TALK ABOUT IT

- Management thinkers regularly stress the importance of "failing" if companies are to grow an entrepreneurial culture, and grow faster. Yet few organizations have sturdy procedures in place to protect those who voluntarily risk failure, or are pushed forward to risk failure. Is your work group consistent in what it claims and what it does to protect those who risk failure on behalf of the organization?

ACT ON IT

- Implement at least one support process that transcends finger pointing and blame, and encourages employees to take intelligent risks—and one process that encourages experimentation. The gains will greatly outweigh the costs.

PERSEVERANCE

"Go back?" he thought. "No good at all!
Go sideways? Impossible!
Go forward? Only thing to do!
On we go!" So up he got, and trotted along
with his little sword held in front of him
and one hand feeling the wall,
and his heart all of a patter and a pitter.
J.R.R. Tolkien, "The Hobbit"

In the early years of World War II, nothing was going right for Britain. Every day brought new setbacks, defeats, and heartbreaks. The island's plight was so severe that Hitler and his inner circle were convinced the British would capitulate. But Britain didn't capitulate, they came roaring back, because in Winston Churchill they had a leader who epitomized perseverance and who didn't believe in giving in.

"If you are going through hell, keep going."
Winston S. Churchill

So Churchill and his beloved Britain went through hell…and kept going. Despite the reverses of Norway and Dunkirk, despite the incessant bombing during the Blitz and enormous loss of planes and men in the Battle of Britain, despite the absence of a single victory of any sort in the win column, every morning, Britain, her people, and her armies showed up, and pressed on. They persevered. They fought on—one day, one mile, one soldier, one airplane, one tank, one battle at a time—until they eventually earned their first major victory in the Battle of Egypt, and turned a corner—*a* corner, not *the* corner. Their toils were not over; they had to continue persevering and fighting. Or, as Churchill put it in his November 10, 1942 "Gleam of Victory" speech:

"Now this is not the end. It is not even the beginning of the end. But it is, perhaps, the end of the beginning."

Leadership journeys are also about beginnings, and moving forward. But the way forward is seldom simple or easy. Like life, leadership journeys are marked by twists and turns, ups and downs. They have their own array of obstacles to tackle, some imposed on them, such as legislation, and others created by them, such as depleted cash stocks caused by the reckless pursuit of global expansion. Even if organizations and leaders are disciplined and meticulous in charting and navigating their leadership journeys, they may not always get the prize they desire, be it operational excellence or market dominance, as context and circumstances invariably have their say. Just as the Bible reminds us in *Ecclesiastes,* the race doesn't always go to the swiftest, or the battle to the strongest, all are subject to time and chance.

Since time and chance have a say in all things (leaders and leadership included), every decision carries within it a test of will and desire. The dynamics that shape this interplay between will and desire can be summarized by three interlinked propositions—how hungry are leaders and organizations to achieve their goals, how much effort are they willing to expend in the pursuit of their desired goals, and for how long are they willing to stay the course, even when repeatedly obstructed or denied. Soulful leaders are aware of this tug-of-war between will and desire. They understand that desire is easy. But, they also understand that desire without the will to *go through hell,* if necessary, to attain their goals is just a hollow. They are acutely aware that the only way they can achieve their desired goals is by staying the course and persevering—just like a river, which doesn't stop flowing each time it runs into rocks and boulders. The river's job is to flow, so it sticks to it and fulfils its purpose by finding a way around the obstructing rocks and boulders. This "stick-to-itiveness," a phrase Thomas Edison—one of the greatest role models for this essay's theme—used frequently, is the spine of perseverance. Each of Edison's unsuccessful attempts to invent the light bulb could be considered a failed attempt. But he didn't quit. He kept going. He persevered. He stuck to his task. He kept flowing till he reached his journey's goal—inventing the light bulb.

Blood, toil, and tears are not exclusive to wartime leadership journeys, or those undertaken by intrepid inventors, they are integral to all leadership journeys. Consequently, soulful leaders expect to be tested. They don't throw up their hands in despair each time they run into rough weather, because intellectually and intuitively they know that no journey worth undertaking is ever easy. If a goal is valuable, it will exact its price in effort and toil, and the grander the vision powering their journey, the greater the difficulties. So they press on in pursuit of bold goals and visions, undeterred by obstacles and difficulties.

Czeslaw Milosz offers valuable advice in this regard to journeying leaders in his poem, "The Accuser." The poem relies on
some of the same words as Robert Frost's poem, "The Road Not
Taken," to convey its message, though Milosz is more explicit in
stating the importance of "confronting difficulty" as a prerequisite
for reaching the castle (a goal, a dream, a destination).

Until you reach the crossroads. There will be two paths.

One difficult and down, another easy and up.

Take the difficult one, simple Johnny. Again two paths.

One difficult and up, another easy and down.

Go up and it will lead you to the castle.

Czeslaw Milosz, "The Accuser"

It's interesting to observe how Milosz reverses the direction of
difficulty. The first time it is difficult and down; the second time,
it is difficult and up. Regardless of the direction, up or down,
only one way leads to the castle—the difficult way. Soulful leaders
don't cringe from difficulties, they embrace them and persevere.

The merits of perseverance have been advocated and upheld
through the ages by thinkers, poets, and leaders alike. In the play,
"Troilus and Cressida," Shakespeare's Ulysses advises Achilles that
"perseverance keeps honor bright." Tennyson expresses a similar
sentiment in his poem, "Ulysses," when he expresses a preference
for *"shining in use,"* over *"pausing and ending."* How true. Because
the only time we can really assess the value of a leader is when
they are shining in use—persevering—not when they are out of
sight, pausing, resting, and rusting. Contemporary leaders, such
as Churchill, Nehru, and Mandela would have agreed with both

Shakespeare and Tennyson. For these leaders, continuous effort was more potent in resolving leadership challenges than strength and intelligence. No matter how many hills they had climbed, there were always more to climb to achieve their goals.

Perseverance is a key feature of soulful leadership for all the reasons discussed thus far in this essay. Ongoing increases in well-being and prosperity are amassed only through sustained effort, and by constantly confronting obstacles and difficulties. However, the merits and value of perseverance notwithstanding, it is easier celebrated than practiced. A few reasons explaining why follow.

First, perseverance requires tons of stamina and energy. And soulful leaders seem to have it, unending stamina and exorbitant amounts of energy. They rise early, work, work, work till late at night, sleep a little, then are up again at the crack of dawn, and back to work. And they bluntly demand that same superhuman stamina from those who are picked, or who volunteer to travel with them. It's as if they were echoing Whitman.

He traveling with me needs the best blood, thews [muscles; physical strength], endurance...
(I and mine do not convince by arguments, similes, rhymes,
We convince by our presence.)
Walt Whitman, "Song of the Open Road"

There are numerous examples of heads of state, politicians, corporate leaders, musicians, artists, writers, journalists, nuns and priests, mothers, fathers, doctors, nurses, caregivers, people from all walks of life who toil tirelessly day after day. The legendary B.B. King, the unofficial King of the Blues, was once asked when he intended to retire. His answer, "the day I die." True to his word he worked, toiled, and performed till the day he died.

Pope John Paul II was called the "The Pilgrim Pope" for a reason. He was one of the most traveled leaders in world history. According to Vatican reports, during his approximately 27 years in office he traveled to 129 different countries, many where no Pope had ever visited, logging close to 750,000 miles—a schedule that would have broken the back of people half his age. Even more jaw dropping if we keep in mind that his schedule didn't include any down time for chilling, surfing, and hanging loose, as most of us would have done (or liked to do).

Mother Teresa may not have been such a globe trotter, but she too lived long, hectic days full of vigor and vitality. The mere thought of rising at 4:30 every day, day in and day out, and carrying on till 10 at night, with minimum rest and breaks, would be daunting for most mortals. Because they demand so much of themselves, soulful leaders are not shy of demanding a lot of others too. It's the cost of affiliation, take it or leave it.

Second, perseverance demands endurance. Fatigue, at least as most ordinary people understand it, doesn't factor in the mix. Military historians attest to this. They report that early battles in most wars are won by speed, surprise, and power. But subsequent battles, and the war as a whole, are won by endurance, relentlessness, and perseverance, the ability and capacity to tirelessly keep going longer than the enemy, to show up every day to fight and slug it out, and eventually wear down the enemy. This is what happened in the Battle of Stalingrad. The Russians refused to quit and outlasted the Germans, wearing down their will to fight and finally causing them to surrender. In this respect, the Russian soldiers embodied the will Kipling describes lyrically in his poem, "If."

If you can force your heart and nerve and sinew
To serve your turn long after they are gone,
And so hold on when there is nothing in you
Except the will which says to them: 'Hold on!'
Rudyard Kipling, "If"

There is also evidence, away from the battlefield, of perseverance winning the war by wearing down the "enemy," be it a colonial superpower or an intractable physics problem. Mahatma Gandhi, a frail, wispy man with boundless energy and endless staying power, was able to win independence for India by persevering with his *satyagraha* movement (non-violent political resistance) and wearing down Britain's will to rule India. Albert Einstein, the genius physicist, exhibited this same staying power when it came to difficult scientific theories and discoveries, claiming, "It's not that I'm so smart, it's just that I stay with problems longer."

Staying with problems longer, stick-to-itiveness, keep going ("through hell," if necessary), different words and phrases but with the same underlying theme and meaning, all connote sustained initiative in the face of unyielding uncertainty. This simultaneously brings two leadership capabilities into play. The first is patience. Not in the passive sense of waiting for good things to happen, but in the sense taught by the proverb, "Rome was not built in a day". Soulful leaders operate with the live realization that many of life's problems can be intransigent, so they are willing to wait and live through the uncertainty of the challenges, without an irascible itch to constantly push the river to flow. Viewed from this perspective, patience is a close relative of what Keats famously called, "Negative Capability."

*"…what quality went to form a Man of Achievement especially in
Literature & which Shakespeare possessed so enormously…I mean
Negative Capability, that is when man is capable of being in uncertainties, Mysteries, doubts, without any irritable reaching after fact
& reason…."*

**Keats, December 1817 letter to brothers George
and Thomas**

Paradoxically, the same leaders who are willing to remain patient, must also be willing to *risk* impatience. True, they remember that "Rome was not built in a day." But, they also recall Chau-
cer's advice:

"Ay fleeth the tyme; (the time will fly), it nyl no man abyde (it
will pause for no man)."

So soulful leaders balance patience and impatience, and make
wise choices concerning when and what to be patient or impatient with, and why, as the following case study demonstrates.

On June 16, 2011, IBM celebrated its 100th birthday. But it
came very close to never getting there. In the early '90s, when Lou
Gerstner took over as CEO, IBM was hemorrhaging cash and on
the brink of bankruptcy. A victim of its own success, the behe-
moth was stuck in the past, horribly attached to business models
and processes that had once produced a glorious era, but were
irrelevant to the market and customers' emerging needs.

Consequently, Gerstner was impatient with factors that kept
IBM chained to its glorious—but no longer potent—past, and
pushed for immediate change to prevent the company from
dying. Specifically, he was impatient with the company's in-
ward-looking focus and obsession with hardware— "Let's stop

ramming steel (mainframes and hardware) down the throats of our customers," —and killed product lines and aggressively cut costs so IBM could stop bleeding cash and survive.

But his perseverance took a gentler, more patient form when it came to transforming the operating culture of the company away from obsessing about technologies and products to serving customer needs, and away from corporate infighting to greater collaboration. It was not that his dogged determination to revive and transform the technology giant wavered. He was acutely aware that companies like IBM, with entrenched histories rich in mythology and beliefs of their own greatness, don't drop their attachments to their storied pasts and change overnight, even when confronted by impending doom. So he was willing to wait longer, and be more patient.

Perseverance is a vital element of soulful leadership. But it's not perseverance ruled by nostalgia and attachments to historical greatness that border on blindness and stubbornness. Nostalgia has no place in a soulful leader's quiver, as the IBM case so deftly demonstrates. The world changes. One era gives way to another—analog to digital, cash to credit cards to electronic money, prepared foods to processed foods, and a lot more. Life moves on, as the ancient Persian poet, Omar Khayyam, gently reminds us:

The Moving Finger writes; and, having writ,
Moves on: nor all thy Piety nor Wit
Shall lure it back to cancel half a Line,
Nor all thy Tears wash out a Word of it.
Omar Khayyam, "The Rubaiyat of Omar Khayyam"

Stopping, refocusing, and redirecting perseverance is equally vital for the practice of soulful leadership. Perseverance in pursuit of visions and goals that have outlived their expiry date diminish the wellbeing and prosperity of companies, rather than increase them. Companies like IBM, Kodak, Dow Chemical, Xerox, HP, Burberrys, Harley-Davidson, Mitsubishi, Bayer, and Birla Industries could have benefited if their leaders had stopped, refocused, and redirected their perseverance, before the ominous threat of corporate demise forced their hand. Consequently, soulful leaders should constantly ask themselves if their perseverance and stick-to-itiveness requires refocusing and redirecting. The capability of perseverance is non-negotiable; its direction is discretionary. An inner awakening guided by the ability to see reality for what it is indispensable in helping leaders decide when to adjust direction and when to refocus.

Some poems were written with one sole purpose, to give and keep giving. The poem, "Don't Quit," attributed to Edgar Guest, is such a poem. Each time our shoulders droop and our head hangs seeing the hills still left to climb, each time our sighs pour lead in our weary feet, each time the blazing heat of effort sears our will and we wonder if we should press on, this old faithful embraces us and fills us with renewed courage to persevere. Its beauty lies not in its lyrical complexity, but in its sincerity. Its simplicity comforts us, and its clarity energizes us. Each time we reach for it, or it reaches for us, the poem whispers to us, in an unassuming way, its eternal truth, its timeless message: "Don't Quit."

When things go wrong, as they sometimes will,

when the road you're trudging seems all uphill,

when the funds are low and the debts are high,

and you want to smile but you have to sigh,

when care is pressing you down a bit - rest if you must, but don't you quit.

Life is queer with its twists and turns.

As everyone of us sometimes learns.

And many a fellow turns about when he might have won had he stuck it out.

Don't give up though the pace seems slow - you may succeed with another blow.

Often the goal is nearer than it seems to a faint and faltering man;

Often the struggler has given up when he might have captured the victor's cup;

and he learned too late when the night came down,

how close he was to the golden crown.

Success is failure turned inside out - the silver tint of the clouds

of doubt,

and when you never can tell how close you are,

it may be near when it seems afar;

so stick to the fight when you're hardest hit –

it's when things seem worst, you must not quit.

Edgar Guest, "Don't Quit"

Edgar Guest and Czeslaw Milosz lived in different eras and obviously didn't know each other. But they both shared an eternal insight concerning perseverance.

And he learned too late when the night came down,

How close he was to the golden crown...

The lines from Guest's poem resonate with and complement the last line below of Milosz's poem, referenced earlier in this essay.

Go up and it will lead you to the castle...

...to the castle, where the golden crown lies! True golden "crowns" are attained only through perseverance, which should make us extremely wary of "crowns" that we celebrate, but have acquired without persevering. Perhaps they are of dubious value. Or worse still, mirages—not gold crowns at all.

THINK ABOUT IT

- How do you fare on perseverance? Especially when things are not going your way and the mounting stress and pressure makes giving in and moving on very tempting? Also think of the times when you soldiered on, regardless of duress and pressure. What are the key factors that made the difference in discouraging perseverance or keeping you going?

TALK ABOUT IT

- How can we as a work group—team, department, division—more effectively nurture a "stick-to-itiveness" culture so budgets and effort aren't rolled back prematurely when markets and customers respond worse than expected?

ACT ON IT

- Organize an organization-wide jam, or some other form of collaborative brainstorming technique, to generate ideas concerning the organization's collective ability to persevere intelligently, and balance patience and impatience. For which specific results and performance outcomes should the organization be patient, and for which should it be impatient?

PERSPECTIVE

If thou of fortune be bereft,
and in thy store there be but left
two loaves, sell one, and with the
dole, buy hyacinths to feed thy soul.
John Greenleaf Whittier

We live in a world that venerates winning and success, and measures them with gains in material wealth—money and things. Organizations too like winning and succeeding. Feeding this fetish is a standing army of folk heroes—sports coaches, famous athletes and artists, decorated armed forces personnel, rich executives and industrialists—who have given winning and succeeding heavenly status through their pithy one-liners: *Winning is everything; Winning is the only thing; The whole world loves a winner (…and has no time for a loser).*

It shouldn't be surprising to learn, therefore, that few characteristics of organizations and humans cause as much stress and grief as this endless pursuit of winning and craving for success. Serious enough for it to destroy families and wreck the mental and physical health of people, and by extension, the wellbeing of the organizations where these people work. Isn't it time we took a good hard look at ourselves in the mirror, and asked ourselves a few truly tough questions?

- What is success? Can it be sustained endlessly?
- Can people appear successful on the outside, yet feel like failures within?
- If people are successful only at work, but not in other parts of their lives, can it really be called success?
- How many hours a day do people need to work every day in the pursuit of success? Do they need to work on weekends too? Even during vacations and holidays?
- And what about money? How much is enough, especially as people's needs, wants, and desires can be limitless?

These are not idle, academic questions. Philosophers and poets, like Robert Service, often called the Canadian Kipling, have been asking these soul-searching questions for ages, because they significantly, and often irreversibly, affect our day-to-day lives, both at home and at work.

> *I wonder if successful men*
> *Are always happy?*
> *...I wonder if a millionaire*
> *Jigs with enjoyment,*
> *...I wonder why so soon forgot*
> *Are fame and riches;*
> **Robert W. Service, "Successful Failure."**

Alfred Adler, who was introduced earlier in the essay on Ego, asks an even more fundamental question: Does success even exist? According to Adler, it doesn't. For him, success is a purely competitive concept, a fixation that robs moment-to-moment living of all joy, since living is deferred to some uncertain time in the future after the individual feels fulfilled by success. Thousands of years ago, the Bhagavad Gita, one of the world's greatest epic poems on self-realization, recognized the destructive pull of rewards and recommended that individuals work for the sake of work, and not for sake of rewards or material gains. Because working for gains is the surest way to breed anxiety and misery. While the advice offered by the Bhagavad Gita is timeless, and endorsed by the wise even today, it is unlikely to attract a sizeable following because a large chunk of contemporary society derives its sense of identity and self-worth through the world of money and things. True, there is more to work than just money and benefits, but for the vast majority, the opportunity for increasing one's material prosperity is the key reason they sacrifice a large part of their lives, their loved ones, and themselves for their jobs.

Which brings us to the threshold of an all-important question: Is all what people sacrifice for their jobs really worth it? Do the gains achieved by winning and succeeding truly compensate for what is lost irretrievably—joy, a life postponed and not lived, and possibly the love of family and friends? Is there another way, or are these sacrifices inevitable in today's possession-dominated world? These are the questions soulful leaders would also ask. Here again, an inner-awakening would help soulful leaders weigh more meaningfully, the gains in material prosperity conferred by winning and succeeding against the sacrifices their people and organizations would have to make to achieve those gains. How they resolve this vital question will be determined by their own humanity, in this case their perspective on what constitutes winning and succeeding, and how much is enough. Regardless of the route they take to balancing gains and sacrifices, soulful leaders rarely forget that winning and succeeding must encompass and fulfill the total human being. No amount of success and prosperity on the outside will ever suffice, if what lives within is a screaming sense of failure. Edwin Arlington Robinson's poem, "Richard Cory," illustrates this in a memorably chilling way.

Whenever Richard Cory went down town,
We people on the pavement looked at him:
He was a gentleman from sole to crown,
Clean favored, and imperially slim.

And he was always quietly arrayed,
And he was always human when he talked;
But still he fluttered pulses when he said,
"Good-morning," and he glittered when he walked.

And he was rich—yes, richer than a king—
And admirably schooled in every grace:
In fine, we thought that he was everything
To make us wish that we were in his place.

So on we worked, and waited for the light,
And went without the meat, and cursed the bread;
And Richard Cory, one calm summer night,
Went home and put a bullet through his head.

Edwin Arlington Robinson, "Richard Cory"

Both poems, "Successful Failures" and "Richard Cory," demonstrate that developing, establishing, and maintaining a perspective on winning and success at work and outside of work is perhaps one of the most important and difficult challenges people face during their lives. Most individuals come to terms with the limitation of this "single-minded pursuit of winning and success at work" model, and are galvanized only when their lives collide head-on with a crisis—suicide, death, divorce, heart attack.

Soulful leaders, though, must act differently. They can't wait for their people and organizations to experience crises and collisions before they swing into action. The people they lead and their organizations expect them to show awareness of this elemental tension between wellbeing and prosperity, then act on that awareness by proactively shaping the work environment so those who work there can experience winning and succeeding both externally and internally. This is the minimum leaders can do to ensure the future wellbeing and prosperity of their people and their organizations. Most people spend the bulk of their lives at work and will break if pushed non-stop in the pursuit of maximizing work-related prosperity. This "breaking" applies to leaders as well. Leaders who are "success-at-work maximizers," will ultimately, no matter how brightly they shine, burn out and, ironically, damage what they pursued most obsessively: prosperity.

So what should soulful leaders do to help their organizations "*recognize and recalibrate*" their perspectives on material success and its relationship with a person's total life, work and non-work. Where should they start?

The most obvious place to start would be work itself, the raison d'être why people show up in the morning. A number of studies, both stand-alone and longitudinal, conducted by organizations, universities, and leading researchers, such as Gallup, Harvard, Daniel Kahneman and Tim Judge, demonstrate that while extrinsic factors (salary and perks) are important, they account for less than 10% of job satisfaction and workplace engagement. For the vast majority, the millennial segment in particular (70-80%), such intrinsic factors as future prospects, learning, and the quality of the work they do is a stronger determinant of job satisfaction and employee engagement. These intangible, non-monetary factors are also important contributors to employees' feelings of accomplishment, feeling valued, and self-worth. More significantly, these intangibles also result in employees feeling successful internally, as they are innately tied to the human longing for meaning, of feeling useful, and of doing work that is *real*.

The work of the world is common as mud.
Botched, it smears the hands, crumbles to dust.
But the thing worth doing well done
has a shape that satisfies, clean and evident.
Greek amphoras for wine or oil,
Hopi vases that held corn, are put in museums
but you know they were made to be used.
The pitcher cries for water to carry
and a person for work that is real.
Marge Piercy, Lines from, "To be of use"

Yes, people like work that is real, as it fosters a sense of "worthiness" and "relevance" to the economic value created by their organizations. This is why growing the integrity and meaningfulness of work across all levels and for all members of the organization, regardless of rank and stature, is often the No. 1 priority of soulful leaders.

An effective strategy that soulful leaders often use toward this end—imbuing work with greater meaning and purpose—is creating forums for connecting employees with end-users, such as customers. Grateful, satisfied, and happy customers are important allies of soulful leaders in making employees feel valued and worthy, since they provide concrete proof of the meaning and value of employees' efforts. Interacting with end-users and customers also builds a positive reinforcement cycle: customers appreciate what employees do for them, which leads to employees developing greater empathy for customers and the desire to provide them with superior quality offerings and experiences, which in turn leads customers to appreciate the organization and employees even more.

The Swedish auto manufacturer, Volvo, was a pioneer in connecting its employees with customers and building this cycle of reinforcement. Employees who built the cars and trucks were also given opportunities to interact with dealers and customers so they could experience, first hand, the appreciation customers expressed for their craftsmanship. Additionally, when customers who had been in car accidents sent unsolicited letters to the company thanking it because the Volvo they were driving had "saved their lives," Volvo sensed an opportunity to imbue work with even more meaning and cause. The company created a club for Volvo drivers who believed that one of the automaker's cars had saved their lives, thereby making employee contributions to their customers' safety more visible. Extremely effective in augmenting the sense of meaning, value, and self-worth among employees, since not much can top *helping save lives by building the safest cars in the world.*

Volvo is not alone in this regard. Leaders at several companies spend a great deal of effort in imbuing work with more meaning and value, by linking everyday work to significant external goals such as preserving family memories (Hallmark Christmas ornaments), nutrition and healthy eating (Whole Foods), and making customers feel like royalty (Singapore Airlines, Emirates, The Ritz-Carlton, Four Seasons). This investment pays for itself several times over and is a proven source of competitive advantage. A Gallup study on the subject demonstrates that employees in diverse economies and cultures, such as Canada, India, Indonesia, Netherlands, Singapore, Thailand, United Arab Emirates, and USA, were more likely to experience a higher-than-average level of success and achievement, both externally and internally, if they also felt enthusiastic and committed to their work and workplace. An outcome that's unlikely to occur if a sense of meaning and value is missing from everyday work.

While worthwhile and significant work undoubtedly is an important contributor to an individual's feeling of success and achievement, it is equally important to remember that humans are complex, multidimensional beings with many varied needs, and work is only one aspect of their lives. Consequently, any discussion of "success" and "meaning" must address a person's total, or whole, life. Since it's impossible for life to feel whole if filled only by work, human beings can't remain lively, vital, and creative—all prerequisites for experiencing success and achievement externally and internally—if they lead predominantly work-centric existences. Just as the sun rises and sets in nature, the sun must rise and set on work so people can actively engage with the non-work aspects of their lives, because they too contribute to a sense of worth and feeling valued.

The poet Longfellow describes this rhythm of work beginning and work ending in his poem, "The Village Blacksmith."

Toiling,—rejoicing,—sorrowing,

Onward through life he goes;

Each morning sees some task begin,

Each evening sees it close;

Something attempted, something done,

Has earned a night's repose.

Henry Wadsworth Longfellow, Lines from, "The Village Blacksmith"

The Blacksmith toils hard and long, but his life is not consumed by work. The sun rises on his work day, and it sets on it, leading to a sense of satisfaction and fulfillment—something attempted, something done. Tragically though, for millions around the world, the sun never really sets on their work. Today's 24x7 perpetually connected e-mail, and device-dominated digital world, often results in people continuing to work even after they have left their workplace. The problem doesn't just exist on the fringes involving only workaholic outliers, it is mainstream and is worrying countries and legislators.

France, for example, is considering a labor reform bill that will require companies of 50 or more employees to limit the spillover of work into the private lives of employees, specifically as it relates to "digital technology." The bill proposes establishing a policy that will specify hours when employees aren't supposed to send or receive email. In an interview with BBC, Benoit Hamon of the French National Assembly captured the essence of the malaise: "Employees physically leave the office, but they do not leave their work. They remain attached by a kind of electronic leash—like a dog. The texts, the messages, the emails—they colonize the life of the individual to the point where he or she eventually breaks down." Regardless of whether legislation passes or is shot down, the significant problems of stress and burn-out will remain, which soulful leaders must confront and resolve.

Elsewhere in Germany, companies, not legislators, are heading the movement. Vehicle maker Daimler Benz has adopted an innovative approach to holiday and vacation emails—it allows employees to automatically delete emails they receive while on vacation, so they don't return to work depressed at the thought of trawling through hundreds of emails containing extinct agendas. Employees around the world are clamoring for their organizations to follow Daimler's lead, so they can limit the encroachment of work into their lives and homes.

Unfortunately, good intentions concerning preventing the colonization of people's lives by work will not produce the desired results unless leaders and their organizations rethink the equation between work and life. According to the current mythology, there is work, and then there is life, which begins only when one leaves work. Not surprisingly, a thriving industry exists for helping people achieve a healthy equilibrium between the two, commonly called "work-life" balance. However, this mantra— "work-life balance"— is flawed, because work is a part of life; it is not distinct and separate from it. So the issue is not one of balancing a part with the whole, it is *integrating and synthesizing* a part—work—with the rest of the parts that comprise a person's total life. Further, the expression work-life balance implies that human beings operate in perpetually incomplete and fractured states; when they show up for work, they leave their "life" selves behind, and when they return to their "lives" their work selves magically disappear. But we know this is not how the world or people operate. Each part, work and non-work, distracts us from being "present" in whatever surrounds us. When we report for work, our "lives"—our problems and joys—tag along, and interfere with our ability to fully participate in generating and experiencing work-related success and achievement. Conversely, when away from work, work-related burdens sneak up on us and increase the totality of our burdens, or diminish the sum of our joys. Time is continuous and makes no such distinctions between work and life, it's all life. As the writer Annie Dillard so pithily reminds us, "How we spend our days is, of course, how we spend our lives." To which we may add, "How we spend our nights is also how we spend our lives." As the essay stated earlier, achieving a healthy equilibrium between *economic work* (productivity) and *unencumbered being* (presence) is one of the hardest things to master. This is why developing, cultivating, and nurturing perspective on how we spend our lives is invaluable, especially on the nature of "unencumbered being."

What is this life if, full of care,
We have no time to stand and stare...
No time to see...squirrels hide their nuts in grass...
No time to see...streams full of stars, like skies at night...
A poor life this if, full of care,
We have no time to stand and stare.
William Henry Davies, Lines from "Leisure"

In its truest form, leaving work mentally and physically is about leisure. It's tragic that prevalent perspectives concerning success and achievement treat work as indispensable religion, but leisure as expendable. Perhaps we've forgotten the true meaning of leisure, and the role it has played in our growth and evolution. Standing and staring and seeing—leisure as described by the poet above—is not a pampered luxury enjoyed by the self-indulgent rich, nor is it the stupor of idleness exhibited by the lazy. Leisure may or may not even be present in things typically associated with it, like personal time, weekends, vacations, and holidays. At its core, leisure is all about self-renewal; it's "non-activity," not "inactivity." It's unencumbered immersion in whatever is in front of us—a yawning baby, the courage of an amputee, a glorious sunrise. Whatever is in front of us totally grips our mind, heart, and senses, and we (and everything else) disappear. These moments of disappearing allow us to see and hear the world differently because of the inner harmony and oneness we experience with the world. As a result, we are filled with fresh vitality and creativity. Poems rise in our hearts, pictures in our mind, new and fresh songs and tunes hum in our heads, as do new resolves and fresh intentions. In his provocative book, "Leisure: The Basis of Culture," philosopher Joseph Pieper presents evidence of this, and reminds us that many of our greatest art, science, philosophy, technology, and medicine originated in leisure—in moments of unencumbered presence and total immersion in reality. Newton, Mozart, Sappho, Blake, Hemmingway, Archimedes, Pasteur, Al-Khwarizmi (father of algebra), Aryabhata (credited with discovering zero) are just a few of the prime examples of fortunes that flow from total immersion in reality.

Leonardo Da Vinci, one of the most diversely talented indi-viduals ever and, arguably, one of the most successful (maybe not by today's materialistic metrics) is an outstanding example of unquenchable curiosity and fierce imagination rooted in leisure, and not in a one-dimensional obsession with work. His life is a testament to the skill and dexterity with which he integrated and synthesized the many aspects of himself. We can all learn from this great teacher.

Every now and then go away
have a little relaxation
for when you come back
to your work
your judgment will be surer;
since to remain constantly at work
will cause you to lose power
of judgment...
Go some distance away
because the work appears smaller
and more of it
can be taken in at a glance
and a lack of harmony or proportion
is more readily seen.
Leonardo Da Vinci

If reconnecting with true leisure in a meaningful and ongoing way is indispensable for creativity and growth, then what can soulful leaders and their organizations do to integrate and synthesize leisure at work? First, like the foundational principle of parenting, they can show keenness for this virtue and model this behavior for the rest of the organization. Numerous opportunities abound. All organizations, regardless of how high their boundary walls, are surrounded by communities with rich and diverse offerings—art, sculpture, pottery, music, literature, doctors and surgeons, architects, school children, yoga and meditation, and dance studios—all capable of captivating us completely and allowing us to experience brief periods of leisure while at work. Imagine how thrilled a group of school children would be if they were given a chance to show off their budding robotic skills to the leadership team of a work-automation company, people their parents' ages or older. Next, imagine the leisure and self-renewal the adults (the company's executives) would experience as they stepped out of their own worlds into the world of these kids exhibiting smarts and skills they themselves didn't possess when they were that young. Any and every opportunity soulful leaders can provide for their people and organizations to step out, completely step out, of their own world, and enter another unfamiliar world during work hours, no matter how briefly, would invite leisure and foster self-renewal—and subsequently greater engagement with work and more creativity in conducting it.

Finally, no discussion on perspective concerning success, achievement, and fulfillment can be complete without answering the fundamental question, "How much success is enough?" Especially as the pursuit of more and bigger dominate the consciousness and operating philosophy of several leaders and their organizations: "Biggering, and Biggering, and Biggering," as The Once-ler boasts to The Lorax, in Dr. Seuss's eponymous book,

The Lorax. Operating philosophies that can be captured by single words, such as, "More", "Bigger", "Greatest," vaporize joy from work; they rarely increase the overall wellbeing and prosperity of people and organizations. That's because the goals these philosophies encourage are often unachievable, or represent dead-end destinations. More what? Sales, customers, profits, acquisitions? More success? More is an ambiguous and unachievable goal, because even when one has achieved it, there is…MORE!

It is important and merits repeating, the pursuit of *more* robs life of even simple joys, and is unsustainable. Which is why soulful leaders deliberately sponsor and cultivate organization cultures that emphasize enough-ness; a mindset that values work-related success and achievement, without sacrificing people's lives. They know and realize that whole individuals—those who engage in self-care and fulfillment on multiple dimensions—are a greater asset to themselves, their co-workers, and their organizations, precisely because they know when to start, when to stop, and when to renew. So they focus relentlessly on developing and nurturing a keen perspective that enables two key contributions toward this end. First, they keep the striving in pursuit of maximizing success and achievement through a single aspect of people's lives—work—in check, so people's lives are not colonized by work. Second, they imbue work with greater relevance and meaning so people can lead more successful and fulfilling lives, both externally and internally.

Strong attachments and beliefs are like prisons. Locked in their hold, we become blind to ideas and philosophies that threaten and challenge our entrenched positions. The sure-fire way of breaking free from this trap is to open the windows of our minds and heart, and actively welcome ideas and philosophies that we, ourselves, may never have considered. For example, the idea and philosophy concerning success that never ever mentions work. Emerson's plainly worded poem does precisely this; it gives us an alternate perspective of success, not by thumping us on the head, but by gently inviting us to consider success in ways that typically we may not. It is presented here with the hope that it will renew us, and by offering an unpretentious way of thinking about success, enable us to arrive at a healthier equilibrium between *economic work* (productivity) and *unencumbered being* (presence).

To laugh often and much

To win the respect of intelligent people and the affection of children

To earn the appreciation of honest critics and endure the betrayal of false friends

To appreciate beauty

To find the best in others

To leave the world a bit better, whether by a healthy child, a garden patch, or a redeemed social condition

To know even one life has breathed easier because you have lived

This is to have succeeded.

Ralph Waldo Emerson, "Success"

THINK ABOUT IT

- Have you taken time to get far from the madding crowd and define what success means to you? Please do. It could be invaluable when life decides to take detours, or doesn't always show up in ways you desire it should.

TALK ABOUT IT

- In your own department or division (or the organization), has the pursuit of MORE—bigger, better, larger, faster—crossed the "red line," meaning rather than adding to the overall well-being and prosperity of the people, it is actually making work and the workplace less enjoyable and meaningful?

ACT ON IT

- Adopt and act on the 95-95 rule in your own immediate work group, it will spread through the rest of the organization because it's contagious. Here's how the rule unfolds:

  * *The pre-requisite*: Forget perfectionism, because at its core, perfectionism stems from insecurity and is all about winning and controlling. It is unattainable and a hostile game.

  * *The First 95*: Accept most things once they are 95% perfect (meaning things are still not perfect, they are imperfectly-perfect, and that's OK).

  * *The Second 95*: Follow the first 95% rule, 95% of the time (just let go at other times).

  * *The Outcome*: Watch your life become 95% better (Why not 100%? Ah, there's the rub. Read the 95-95 rule again).

BEYOND THE LEADER'S WORLD

ORBITING IN WIDER CIRCLES

No man is an island,
Entire of itself
John Donne, "No Man Is An Island"

In the pantheon of love and metaphysical poets, John Donne has few equals. His poems speak as freshly to us today as they did when he first wrote them, approximately four hundred years ago. His simple line, "No man is an island," provokes us to think deeper about the web of life, the connections that we have with the universe beyond ourselves that offer us a way of completing ourselves.

Soulful leaders have heard John Donne, because intellectually and emotionally they recognize that organizations and institutions aren't islands either. Neither are leaders and their leadership journeys. Their existences and identities are interwoven and interdependent with realities that extend beyond them—social, cultural, political, environmental—of which they are a part, and in which they operate. The obviousness of these connections and interdependencies notwithstanding, leaders and organizations haven't always been quick to embrace them and act on them.

Historically, commercial organizations have given top priority to their own economic interests. Yet, there have been exceptions. Examples of companies—years ahead of their times—that have recognized the interdependence between protecting and promoting their commercial interests and furthering the wellbeing and prosperity of the communities in which they operated include the following:

- Cadbury of UK upgraded and improved working and living conditions and wages for its employees by moving its factory to a "cleaner, healthier" site, Bournville, in the late 1870s.

- Eastman Kodak, a pioneering giant of photography, had several enlightened worker-centric practices in place in the 1920s, such as profit-sharing, sickness benefits, pension plan, and accident insurance.

- In India, Tatas, also a pioneering company, built an entire township, Jamshedpur, in the early part of the 20th century, for its workers and staff, with schools, hospitals, and other vital social necessities not readily available in those times.

- In 1943, Robert Wood Johnson, one of the founders of Johnson & Johnson, developed the company's credo, stating that its primary stakeholders were customers, employees, and the communities in which it operates (in that order).

The enlightened nature of the above practices notwithstanding, for the vast majority of commercial organizations in the 19th and 20th centuries, the profit motive was the single biggest goal of executive leadership. Money, size, and scope conferred upon them unrivaled power and clout, which they willingly used for their own benefit. There was little countervailing power as most governments were in cahoots with big business; the phrase "crony capitalism" may be of recent vintage, but the phenomenon has thrived for ages. The profit motive, or shareholder value as it is fashionably called today, had many allies and was kept strong and vital by periodic booster shots administered by heavyweight profit prophets, like Nobel Prize winning economist, Milton Friedman: "The social responsibility of business is to increase profits. The businessmen...not concerned merely with profit but also with promoting desirable social ends...providing employment, eliminating discrimination, avoiding pollution and whatever else may be the catchwords of the contemporary crop of reformers...are preaching pure and unadulterated socialism."

Consequently, interests and needs of organizations and communities that did business with these powerful companies had few champions. Those that dared make their voices heard were frequently dismissed as muckrakers. Well-intentioned reformers, such as Ralph Nader (American activist known for supporting consumer protection, environmentalism, and government reform causes) and others like him, have never quite enjoyed the same stage and spotlight as flamboyant CEOs and their muscular organizations, even when their arguments and ideas were obviously better and had the power of benefitting the greater many.

Let's not fool ourselves. The pull of the profit motive has not weakened over the decades. Fortunately, however, it has been tempered by a growing realization that organizations are not islands, and they do need to pay more than mere lip service to the interdependencies they share with the environments in which they operate. Society and governments have also become more demanding and are setting more stringent standards and expectations concerning the manner in which organizations, large or small, local or global, manage their self-interests relative to the interests of others that exist, work, and play in the ecosystems in which they operate. Consequently, leadership journeys that rely heavily on profit-maximizing activities, such as firing employees, selling shoddy products, and polluting the environment, are increasingly being frowned upon and legislated against, since they cause real and irreversible harm to the wellbeing and prosperity of the environments in which leaders and their leadership journeys take place.

Highly visible forums like the UN 2030 Agenda for Sustainable Development, World Economic Forum, and World Business Council for Sustainable Development, are also involved in furthering a broader, "beyond-profit" agenda. Burning issues confronting our world, such as global warming and income inequality (people at the bottom-of-the pyramid are still around), have given rise to a new breed of business leaders, like Paul Polson (CEO Unilever), Richard Branson (CEO Virgin Enterprises), and John Mackay (CEO Whole Foods) who are committed to restoring faith in big business by practicing conscious capitalism, and demonstrating that business can be a force of good for the wellbeing and prosperity of worlds beyond their own, such as employees, customers, communities, cultures and nationalities, and above all, the health of our planet.

This tempering and transformation has given rise to a whole new vocabulary and mindset for assessing progress and measuring performance. Some examples of this new vocabulary and new measures of a world beyond profit include:

- Sustainable development—comprising economic development, social inclusion, environmental protection, and cultural diversity

- Triple bottom line (TBL)—not just profits, but people, planet, and profits

- Corporate Social Responsibility (CSR)—verifiable commitment to operating in a sustainable manner as described above

- Conscious capitalism—an approach to doing business that attempts to serve humanity and multiple stakeholders engaged with businesses

These pillars of "beyond-profit" consciousness have also spawned a slew of new measuring and performance reporting systems duly backed by appropriate awards and accolades. Companies like Unilever, Royal Dutch Shell, Kao, Levi's, and Mahindras routinely report on their sustainable development achievements. And annually, highly visible and touted awards like Dow Jones Sustainability Index Award recognize and celebrate companies at the forefront of sustainable development.

Undeniably, there is visible and tangible progress on issues like sustainability and social responsibility, but it has yet to achieve the status of a sustained and widespread movement. A sizeable journey still lies ahead before businesses and other social institutions can unequivocally demonstrate, through their actions, that *they exist for the good of the economy and the planet, and not the other way around.* Our world needs more than just a few front runners.

The woods are lovely, dark and deep,

But I have promises to keep,

And miles to go before I sleep,

And miles to go before I sleep.

Robert Frost, "Stopping By Woods On A Snowy Evening"

Yes, we have miles to go before we can be assured that businesses are adequately fulfilling their obligations to meeting the needs of worlds beyond their own. Globally, many businesses are still producing and consuming at rates that are unsustainable; they still put profits and their own interests over those of all others. For instance, the global economic meltdown of 2008 played havoc with the lives of people around the world, yet the culture of wanton greed that caused it is still alive and rampant. The "Occupy Wall Street" movement may have run out of parks and lost its army of protestors, but the issues they were protesting—income inequality, political corruption, and the influence of big business on government priorities and policies (crony capitalism)—still exist. The success of Bernie Sanders' overt and undisguised socialist campaign in the 2016 US primary elections in the Mecca of Capitalism corroborates that the angst stakeholders harbor against big businesses and crony capitalism is real.

There is a wise aphorism that advises, "Wherever there's angst, there's also opportunity." Accordingly, it is in pursuit of opportunity that this book transitions to the next three essays, in which we'll explore how soulful leaders can accelerate and scale this transformation from business mainly for profit to "business as a force of good" for people, communities, and the planet.

Every era poses new challenges and demands that can be met only if society – individuals and organizations – rids itself of the tyranny of dead ideas, and rises to the occasion by thinking and acting in novel and impactful ways. Charles de Gaulle once declared with characteristic flair, "Big people don't splash around in shallow water." Soulful leaders would do themselves credit by being "big people," trading in "big ideas." Running a business for profit is by no means a dead idea, because a defunct business is of no use to anybody. However, "business as a force for the larger good" is definitely the bigger idea. It's in these bigger ideas and deeper waters that soulful leaders can, and should, make significant contributions.

Part of this bigger idea is helping others achieve higher levels of wellbeing and prosperity.

If I can stop one heart from breaking,
I shall not live in vain;
If I can ease one life the aching,
Or cool one pain,
Or help one fainting robin
Unto his nest again,
I shall not live in vain.
Emily Dickinson

Connecting with, and helping others achieve "higher levels of wellbeing and prosperity" benefits both the giver and the receiver. It helps people feel more fulfilled, more worthy, more assured that they haven't lived in vain, which is why soulful leaders encourage their people and organizations to connect and engage with "worlds beyond their own."

Finally, we return to where we started, the theme of connectedness. No man is an island, leaders and organizations included. The three essays that follow have a unifying theme, a big idea worthy of soulful leaders. Best captured by the African word "Ubuntu," it is the theme of connected consciousness: "I am because we are." Consequently, the wellbeing and prosperity of organizations, leaders, and leadership journeys are intertwined with the worlds they are connected with, but that lie beyond their own. We may never reach the ideal of Ubuntu, but that's not a good reason for staying put, and not trying.

I live my life in widening orbits
that reach out across the world.
Perhaps I may never achieve the last one
Yet, that will be my attempt.
Rainer Maria Rilke, Lines from, "Book of Hours"

The wellbeing and prosperity of the greater many can increase, but only if leaders heed the highly acclaimed German poet-philosopher Rilke's urging, and circle over the worlds in which they operate in ever-widening orbits. It's one of the strongest ways of expressing solidarity with the ideas and practice of soulful leadership.

FIRST ORBIT: EMPLOYEES AND CUSTOMERS

We do not believe in ourselves until someone reveals
that something deep inside us is valuable, worth listening to,
worthy of our trust, sacred to our touch.

e.e. cummings

A few years ago, Vineet Nayyar, the colorful former CEO of HCL Technologies, and a man with fervent opinions, published a book, *Employees First, Customers Second.* While he was not the first CEO to have honored employees, and put them on a pedestal (scores of CEOs have done so for decades), the provocative title explicitly giving precedence to employees over customers forced armies of executives to stop and debate. One faction agreed, "We can see why." Another faction objected, "Why not customers first?"

Employees first, or customers first?

The secret sits in the middle and knows
We dance around in circles and suppose.
Robert Frost, "The Secret"

No secret, the answer is obvious: both employees *and* customers come first. Debating who comes first is ignoring reality and akin to dancing around in circles. Here's why. Imagine the organization as a bird, and employees and customers as the bird's wings. Asking which comes first is like asking which wing of the bird comes first as it flies through the air. Just like a bird needs two wings to fly, organizations prosper only when both come first, i.e., when organizations have committed and enthusiastic employees *and* committed and enthusiastic customers. Soulful leaders know this truth intuitively. Take The Ritz-Carlton, for example, a company universally acknowledged for doing well with both employees and customers. The hotel's motto is: "We are Ladies and Gentlemen serving Ladies and Gentlemen." Where would one set of Ladies and Gentlemen be without the other? The hotel doesn't dance around in circles debating which set of Ladies and Gentlemen comes first; they know both sets need each other to meet their respective needs and feel valued, so they equate their worth using the same words of respect for both in their motto.

Scholarly research and practitioner articles also support this notion that employees and customers bolster each other. Employees who feel valued by their organizations are more likely to exert effort in making customers feel welcome and valuable. Customers are more likely to do business with companies whose employees make them feel more wanted and valued. This virtuous cycle results in happier and more engaged employees, and happier and loyal customers; Vineet Nayyar's book has a similar sentiment at heart. He was not banishing customers to the back of the bus; on the contrary, he was focusing the entire organization's attention on them by focusing on the employees who serve them.

Yet, despite the obvious importance of employees and customers for the current and future health of organizations, instances of organizations treating employees and customers as second class citizens are fairly common. Both sets of people represent a cost, and therefore are frequently sacrificed and subordinated to the needs of material and monetary gain. This makes it even more vital for soulful leaders to ensure that their organizations treat the wellbeing and prosperity of employees and customers as inseparable from their own. What then should soulful leaders do to breathe life into this intent and make it reality? Exactly as e.e. cummings advises at the beginning of the essay. By believing and listening, by caring and paying attention, so others feel valuable and worthy. The remainder of this essay will examine how.

EMPLOYEES

In the visionary science fiction TV series *Star Trek*, William Riker, the Captain's First Mate, frequently asks for "Permission to speak freely, Sir" before addressing his Captain, Jean-Luc Picard. Riker's request, appropriate for dramatizing encounters between two headstrong commanding officers, is also important for the theme of this essay because it epitomizes the plight of millions of employees around the world. They are denied the opportunity to speak freely. Either because their leaders and bosses are intolerant of dissent, and consequently aren't interested in entertaining thoughts, opinions, and ideas contrary to their own. Or because people fearing victimization don't give themselves permission to speak freely: their leaders and bosses wield more power and can damage their jobs and careers if they don't like or approve of what they have to say. What makes matters worse is that even when employees are *invited* to speak freely, it is difficult to tell whether they are speaking words that are their own (meaning they are saying what they truly want to say), or are they merely being "politically correct," speaking in tongues and tones they believe others want to hear.

Denying oneself, or another, the permission to speak freely is a denial of freedom and hence akin to slavery (mental), as James Lowell so eloquently addresses in his poem, "A Stanza on Freedom."

THEY are slaves who fear to speak...
...Rather than in silence shrink
From the truth they needs must think;
They are slaves who dare not be
In the right with two or three.
James Russell Lowell, Lines from,
"A Stanza on Freedom"

Idealism, heroic courage, and daring to speak freely, no matter the odds, are laudable virtues, but flourish more in Lowell's poem than in the everyday world of work. Employees are not martyrs or activists, that's not what they signed up for. It's not fair to expect, or ask, them to sacrifice themselves. The fear of losing one's job, being replaced or kicked aside, or having future prospects—raises, bonuses, promotions—blocked or denied are real and tangible, as are the everyday pressures of supporting families, paying monthly bills, and maintaining a desired lifestyle. The astute question is not why employees shrink from speaking freely. The astute, and only, question is, why aren't workplaces more free and inviting? What prevents leaders and leadership from rolling back these repressive forces of fear and power-induced conformity, so employees can speak more freely, if able? Fettered by fear of reprisal and the insidious demands of toeing-the-party-line, can organizations ever be vibrant, curious, and entrepreneurially creative? And if they can't, can employees be blamed for labeling their workplace as "soulless and dehumanizing?"

Soulful leaders should constantly be thinking about these questions and issues. Even a cursory reading of history demonstrates that fear is a weak platform for launching leadership journeys. Social and political institutions decay when fear denies constituents a voice—especially those who speak and think differently. This is why all societies that cherish "freedom" embrace forms of government that encourage strong opposition to their elected leaders. Through a legitimized system of constructive challenges and criticism, "opposing voices" are expected to keep the elected leaders honest and committed to their mandate, which is why the opposition in the British parliamentary system of democracy is referred to as the "loyal opposition." They are loyal to a higher cause, not merely to ousting the incumbent party and grabbing power for themselves. That both elected leaders and their opposition frequently forget this fundamental tenet is unfortunate. However, that's a topic for a separate essay.

On first reading, Lowell's "Stanza on Freedom" presents itself as an indictment of individuals. Deeper reflection, however, reveals that it is also a cannonade on an organization's systems, culture, and leaders. Literally and figuratively, denying people a voice makes organizations spineless and weak-kneed. Accordingly, the single biggest gift soulful leaders can give their employees is banishment of the fear of speaking freely in the workplace. Because nothing says "We care about our employees" louder than the willingness to truly hear what employees have to say.

By cultivating and nurturing a culture where permission to "speak freely" is a standing entitlement—virtually part of the employment contract with every employee—soulful leaders also send another important message to their employees, "You are worthy and valuable." This feeling of worth, value, and the belief that leaders are interested in what they have to say is what makes employees with different goals, dispositions, temperaments, and personalities want to work together as one organization (cling together in one society), as the poet William Wordsworth so eloquently expresses.

Like harmony in music...
Inscrutable workmanship that reconciles
Discordant elements, makes them cling together
In one society.
William Wordsworth, Lines from, "The Prelude"

The feeling of community and harmony that flows from permission to speak freely is also a compelling invitation for employees to actively engage with work and the workplace, and contribute to creating a future destiny for the organization. It is impossible for employees who feel valued and worthy, and who have a voice, to sit passively on the sidelines. Perhaps the ideal model of "everybody matters," universal participation, or *politeia* that existed in ancient Athens, is out of reach in today's complex world. But surely the "roundtable" model, King Arthur's famous innovation, is not that far-fetched, especially given the pervasiveness of today's connected and collaborative technologies. The roundtable enabled King Arthur to eliminate cumbersome hierarchy and give his knights a voice, so he could "reconcile discordant elements and agendas into one society," and fulfil his dream of creating a united England.

Soulful leaders should aim to do the same in today's non-Camelot work world so they can invite all employees to engage and actively participate in creating wellbeing and prosperity for the organization. In his provocative book, *King Arthur's Roundtable*, renowned Harvard Professor of Education, David Perkins, suggests that roundtables make organizations smarter because, by fostering collaboration, they make pooling mental effort easier. In a manner of speaking, employees are able to put their heads together to sustain the forward momentum of leadership journeys without cracking skulls. A handful of companies, like Cisco, recognize and acknowledge the importance of "clinging together in one society," and have made collaboration the cornerstone of their leadership journeys. Better insights and productive ideas, after all, have never been only the privilege of the most senior and highest paid executives. The story of King Arthur, the boy who lifted the sword from the stone, is proof positive that the wisdom needed to make leadership journeys work for the greater good often comes from unexpected sources.

CUSTOMERS

As with employees, organizations and their leaders like saying to their customers, "We care about you" and "Your business matters to us." Customers hear the words, but don't always believe them. They've seen, heard, and experienced how auto companies (brakes and safety bags), drug companies (drug safety, drug prices), and financial companies (mortgages, usurious interest rates, and hidden charges buried in the fine print), to name a few, have frequently sacrificed them for their own material gain—reducing costs and boosting profits. To make matters worse, in several of these instances where customers' interests were blatantly ignored or sacrificed by powerful global giants, the leaders were complicit, even though publicly they often feigned ignorance. Naturally, customers have become cynical of organizations' claiming how valuable they (and their business) are to them. They interpret those claims as, "our wallets matter, but we, as human beings, people with unique needs, wants, and desires, don't."

Sadly, several leaders share this cynicism. Lou Gerstner, the former CEO of IBM, who saved the tech giant from extinction, admits that for most companies "customers matter" is a mere slogan. Academics and thought leaders agree with Gerstner; many organizations use all the right words when it comes to customers, but fall short in walking that talk. Considering how vital customers are to the existence of organizations, nothing can be simpler, or more obvious, than the maxim, "Without a customer, there is no business." Clearly, soulful leaders can play a significant role in reversing customers' cynicism and in making them feel valued and worthy.

Our focus here is not to advise leaders and their organizations on how they can and should cultivate and grow their relationships with customers; hundreds of marketing books and articles already exist for that purpose. Rather, the goal is to explore a few initiatives that soulful leaders can and should implement to ensure that, in pursuing customers – their business and their wallets – their organizations don't forget that customers are human beings first.

Out of sight, out of mind is as true for customers as it is in everyday human relationships. It's easy to overlook customer interests since they rarely are in the room when organizations make strategic decisions that affect both their wellbeing and prosperity. Consequently, the first thing soulful leaders can (and should) do is to make *the invisible customer highly visible up and down the organization*. Out of sight, yes, but out of mind, definitely not. By fostering a living, breathing culture of "it's all about the customer," soulful leaders can elevate concern and empathy for customers as human beings, which can prevent—or at least strongly discourage—their organizations from pursuing their own wellbeing and prosperity at the expense of customers.

An effective way of giving customers a palpable presence up and down the organization, and hence a voice, is by appointing customer champions in various departments, whose sole job is to ensure that customer interests are kept in sharp focus as leaders plot the forward movement of their leadership journeys. Effectively, these customer champions become vehicles for first importing, then broadcasting, "voices-of-customers" throughout the entire organization. The specific strategy and tactics leaders and organizations implement to achieve this will vary from one organization to the next. The pertinent and important point is that soulful leaders need to lead this charge. If they don't, a "customers matter" consciousness will remain a slogan. Lou Gerstner led the charge by blowing up IBM's attachment to computer hardware and fostering a customer-solutions culture in which IBM-ers acted based on what customers needed, not based on the inventory in the warehouse. A.G. Lafley, the former CEO of Proctor & Gamble (P&G), led the charge by declaring the customer to be the "Boss," and using customers' needs and voices as a magnetic force to galvanize the company and "reconcile the discordant elements of his organization into one *customer-focused* society." Jeff Bezos, CEO of Amazon, leads the charge in his company, albeit with a dash of flair. In meetings, he leaves an empty chair at the table, symbolizing the customers' presence and voice (a practice I have embraced unabashedly and enthusiastically, often dressing the chair with culture-appropriate apparel, like a jacket, t-shirt, cricket or baseball cap, which makes the customer's presence and voice a little more conspicuous and real).

Another contribution soulful leaders can make toward making customers feel valuable and worthy is by fixing the leakiest bucket, the most broken operation in most organizations—customer service. Because nothing that organizations do or say shouts "customers matter" louder than the way in which organizations serve their customers. And the majority of them barely make passing grade. The facial expressions, tone of voice, and general demeanor of most organizations' customer service agents and departments suggest that customers are a bother, a bunch of unwelcome intruders. The cover of Emily Yellin's book, *Your Call Is (Not That) Important to Us*, dramatizes this sentiment with a telling visual. It shows an old-fashioned black telephone with its cord frayed and severed, which appears to shriek, "Customers, please don't call, we don't want to hear from you." Not surprising that customers balk when they hear organizations and their leaders say, "We value our customers." Even less surprising that encounters with these customer service agents and departments leave customers frustrated and drained of any wellbeing they may have been experiencing prior to that encounter. Instead of feeling better and satisfied by being served, customers hang up with "customer service" feeling exasperated, frustrated, and exhausted.

The handful of giants who get it right—Zappos, Four Seasons, Singapore Airlines, Credit Suisse, FedEx, The Ritz Carlton, USAA—truly, madly, deeply care about their customers. These organizations treat serving the customer not as a cost, but as an investment in their own future wellbeing. Intellectually and emotionally service is about human interactions, about treating customers who are human beings as human beings, not as machines; about paying attention to them, not ignoring them; about attending to their needs; and about putting the customer first, not last. In short, giants committed to service, or as Zappos likes to say, "Powered by Service," invest in people and systems that elevate the claim, "Dear customers, your business matters," from a mere slogan to a living breathing reality.

Employees and customers, like the two wings of a bird, are both vital for organizations to prosper. They feed off each other. When employees feel valued and worthy, they win and customers win—because employees who feel valued and worthy are more committed to creating wellbeing and prosperity for their customers and for themselves. When customers are heard and served, they win and employees win. Ask employees in any part of the world, who would they rather work with, happy and satisfied customers, or disgruntled and dissatisfied customers? You know the answer. Additionally, customers trust organizations that value them. As a result, they do more business with those organizations, stay with them longer, and share their happy experiences with others. Because at the end of the day, customer service sensitive to the needs of the customer is still a rarity. It's a win-win because both wings of the bird benefit, and the organization soars.

Underlying this desire for win-win, making both employees and customers feel valuable and worthy, is a profoundly game-changing belief. Soulful leaders view employees and customers as "assets," and treat them as such. They invest in them, and grow the value and future wellbeing and prosperity of these assets. This is also the reason they give them a voice and serve them. The rest have a different belief and mindset. They treat employees and customers as costs, and since costs are always cut, they are more willing to sacrifice employees and customers if it favors increasing their own wellbeing and prosperity.

It's difficult for *one* poem to adequately represent the themes discussed in this essay, but *four short pieces* can.

First, a reminder that we live in complex and uncertain times, in which technological and social advances are inevitable and irrepressible.

It's just that our advances are irrepressible...
I'm not saying it should be this way.
All this new technology
will eventually give us new feelings
that will never completely displace the old ones
leaving everyone feeling quite nervous
and split in two.

David Berman, Lines from "Self-Portrait At 28"

The unpredictability and ambiguity accompanying these "irrepressible" advances leave both employees and customers feeling "quite nervous," making it even more important for soulful leaders to sponsor caring cultures and environments that pay greater attention to the needs of employees and customers, so this nervousness can be soothed.

Next, some sage advice concerning the importance of speaking our truths quietly and clearly, and listening to others' truths.

Speak your truth quietly and clearly;
and listen to others,
even the dull and the ignorant;
they too have their story.
Max Ehrmann, Lines from, "Desiderata"

Yes, all voices—loyalists, cynics, believers, and doubters—all have their stories. Like nutrients, they contribute collectively to building organizational intelligence, which is why soulful leadership demands that leaders work diligently at seeking and liberating diverse voices of employees and customers within their organizations. Insulating leadership journeys from these voices reduces the overall wellbeing and prosperity of all involved with that journey.

Finally, back to e.e. cummings at the top of this essay.

"We do not believe in ourselves until someone reveals
that something deep inside us is valuable, worth listening to,
worthy of our trust, sacred to our touch.
Once we believe in ourselves we can risk curiosity, wonder,
spontaneous delight or any experience that reveals the human spirit."

By treating employees and customers as assets, soulful leaders help them feel worthy and believe in themselves. This emergent self-belief encourages them to risk curiosity and wonder, and spontaneous delight, all potent drivers in increasing the wellbeing and prosperity of all connected with these soulful leadership journeys.

THINK ABOUT IT

- Do you have a regular investment regimen for improving and enhancing your listening skills? What more should you do? Listening is a core leadership skill, and one of the most powerful investments you can make in liberating the voice of employees and the voice of the customer.

TALK ABOUT IT

- It's one thing to claim that employees and customers are assets, it's another to actually treat them as such. Where does your department stand on this issue—on what aspects does it excel and where does it fall short in treating employees and customers as assets?

ACT ON IT

- *Employees*: In your own little corner at work, implement at least one initiative, tomorrow, to liberate the voice of those who work with you, so they don't have to seek permission to speak freely.

- *Customers*: This time not just in your little corner at work, but in the whole organization, become a crusader for "fixing" customer service. Nothing says, "Your business is not that important to us," louder than broken service. Customers want to be served. You'd be doing them a huge favor if you could become a crusader for designing and delivering compelling and memorable customer service and experiences.

SECOND ORBIT: COMMUNITIES

I am forever walking upon these shores,
Betwixt the sand and foam.
The high-tide will erase my footprints,
And the wind will blow away the foam.
But the sea and the shore will remain…
Kahlil Gibran, "Sand and Foam"

As leaders circle in wider orbits beyond the places they live and work, they discover their neighbors, a variety of communities within which they operate—local, global, and even virtual, in today's digital age. These neighbors (communities) are often vastly poorer in resources and skillsets, and beset with a host of problems—illiteracy, teen pregnancies, domestic violence, and drug abuse, to name a few—that have little or no connection with the key goals of their leadership journeys. What should leaders do? Should they stop and help, or should they put on their blinders and pass them by, intent only on navigating their own life's journey? Do leaders and their organizations have any responsibilities and obligations to these communities? Undoubtedly, there are many who must wonder behind closed doors, or in the privacy of their own minds, why paying taxes and being law abiding isn't enough. After all, isn't that what most good citizens do? Must they do more, must they get involved with the myriad of problems experienced by the communities within which they operate?

The parable of the good Samaritan provides an inspiring and instructive starting point for answering these questions. In the biblical tale, before the Samaritan happened upon the traveler who had been robbed, beaten, and left half-dead by the side of the road from Jerusalem to Jericho, a priest and a Levite (literally, a member of the Hebrew tribe of Levi—a relatively well-to-do person in the fable) had already passed by and not stopped to help. Yes, incredible as it may seem, a man of God had not stopped (happens even today). So why did the lowly Samaritan stop and help the unfortunate traveler? What did he see that they didn't?

This is how Martin Luther King, Jr. explained it in his "I've been to the Mountaintop" speech:

The question which the priest and the Levite asked was: "
If I stop to help this man, what will happen to me?"
But...the good Samaritan reversed the question:
"If I do not stop to help this man, what will happen to him?"

Many leaders and organizations don't stop, even though they are aware of the problems faced by the communities that house their operations. Some don't feel the need to, and others feel uneasy about what they might lose if they stop, like the priest and the Levite in the parable. Fortunately, soulful leaders and their organizations do stop and help. Like the Samaritan, they frame the issue differently. They don't ask, "Can we afford to stop and help?" They ask instead, "Can we afford not to stop and help?" This distinction between "afford to" and "afford not to", while semantically slight, can in real life be the difference between life and death. The case of two organizations, Union Carbide and The Tata Group, operating in one country, India, grimly demonstrates this.

The Union Carbide Bhopal poisonous gas tragedy is universally regarded as the world's worst industrial disaster. On the night of December 2, 1984, an accident at the company's pesticide plant in Bhopal leaked a host of toxic gases in the air, including over 30 tons of deadly MIC (methyl isocyanate). The gas cloud spread through the *basti*—a shantytown community inhabited by poor people—causing people's eyes, throats, and skin to burn, inducing nausea and eventually killing thousands. Government figures estimate that more than 15,000 people have died over the years from exposure to the gas. Many who were exposed to the gas on that fateful night have given birth to physically and mentally disabled children. More than 30 years later, the soil and the water table remain contaminated.

How did Union Carbide respond? Like the priest and the Levite, Union Carbide did not stop to help. Even though they were responsible, their leadership decided they couldn't afford to help, so they went on their merry way. The company never formally apologized, and the monetary compensation doled out—significantly less than a billion dollars—is a pittance compared to the multi-billion dollar settlements routinely witnessed in similar cases, like Valdez and Gulf of Mexico oil spills.

Warren Anderson, Union Carbide's global CEO at the time, and his team sought refuge in a rigged and soulless legal system tailored to protect the rich and privileged, at the expense of the less fortunate. That the *basti* dwellers were residents of a third-world country—as India was called at that time (and still is, in many circles)—only made it easier. What is especially stunning and tragically ironic about Union Carbide turning its back on the community is that dozens of its employees and their families lived in the same *basti* that was devastated by the poisonous gas leak. For Union Carbide that was irrelevant, as it probably thought of and treated its employees as a resource—dispensable and consumable. Till the end, the company failed to accept culpability, insisting that the incident was not an accident, but rather an act of sabotage by a rogue worker. The movie, *Bhopal: A Prayer for Rain*, captures Carbide's callousness in one small gut-wrenching scene in which Martin Sheen, playing CEO Warren Anderson, shrugs and smugly declares, "They have no one to blame but themselves," thereby absolving Union Carbide, and himself, of all blame, liability, and obligation to stop and help.

Contrast this with the soulful behavior of Ratan Tata (doyen and the global face of the Tata empire) and his managers following the horrific terror attack on the company's iconic flagship hotel, the Taj Mahal Palace and Tower (known simply as Taj Bombay to millions around the world). On the night of November 26, 2008 (referred to as 26/11 in India), 10 heavily armed Lashkar-e-Taiba terrorists (an Islamic militant organization based in Pakistan) entered Mumbai by sea to attack select targets, including the Taj hotel. The terrorists killed 159 people and wounded 211 across the city in the carnage that followed over the next three days; 34 people were killed and 28 injured in the siege of the Taj.

How did Ratan Tata and his team respond? Like the Samaritan, they stopped and helped because they "couldn't afford not to…" The initiatives implemented by Ratan Tata and his team to help both the community within (the employees) and the community surrounding the Taj (policemen, street vendors, and others) are too numerous to list here. Only a few soul-stirring examples are provided.

- Employees:

  1. All deceased members of the Taj family received monetary settlement, plus full last salary for life for family and dependents.

  2. Fully-paid education of children and dependents—anywhere in the world.

  3. Full medical coverage for whole family and dependents for the rest of their lives.

  4. All loans and advances were waived off—irrespective of amount.

  5. A psychiatric counselor was provided for each person, for life.

- Community surrounding the hotel:

  1. Injured community members—railway employees, street vendors, police staff, and pedestrians—people who had nothing to do with the hotel were provided compensation for six months.

  2. Street vendors whose carts were destroyed were given new carts.

  3. A grand-daughter of a street vendor who caught four bullets was moved from the Government hospital to Bombay Hospital, a private and better-equipped hospital, for better treatment and quicker recovery. Of course, the Tatas covered all the expenses.

The Tata group of companies, and its leaders—members of the family and the senior leadership team—have over a century-old reputation as model employers and first-rate corporate citizens. The very first clause of the conglomerate's operating motto states: "The Tata Group is committed to benefit the economic development of the countries in which it operates. No Tata company shall undertake any project or activity to the detriment of the wider interests of the communities in which it operates." But what the Tata company did in the wake of 26/11 sets a new gold standard for what companies should do in "the wider interests of the community," even when not remotely culpable, or required by law. When the HR team nervously presented a rich compensation and welfare plan for the terror attack's victims, Ratan Tata didn't ask, "Can we afford to?" He asked, instead, "Do you think we are doing enough?"

Helping communities cope with their problems, whether imposed on them by a crisis or otherwise, bears the unmistakable stamp of soulful leadership. Every single day, scores of humanitarian and relief agencies, philanthropists, and social entrepreneurs work tirelessly to increase the wellbeing and prosperity of communities. This book and the author salute them; we are truly blessed for their presence and their mission. But this essay is not about them, and therefore does not cite case studies of their work. This essay is about how everyday organizations, both commercial and nonprofit entities like hotels, banks, trade associations, drug companies, and telecommunication providers, stop and intentionally deploy their specialized knowledge, unique skills, and core competencies to help resolve some of the problems plaguing their communities. The focus of this essay is also not on philanthropy and/or volunteerism that soulful leaders and their organizations pursue in their own free time, but on the activities they perform during their day jobs, activities that integrate and align the objectives of helping communities with their own work goals.

Typically, the help organizations provide to increase the well-being and prosperity of the communities in which they operate fall in one of four categories:

1. Life and career skills development

2. True Empowerment (economic, educational, social, nutritional)

3. Asset Creation (homes, hospitals)

4. Alliances and partnerships for creating unprecedented well-being, like health, sanitation, power, and drinking water

The rest of this essay will present a single case study from each category to illustrate how a few exemplary organizations are integrating their desire to solve community problems with their own operating goals.

LIFE AND CAREER SKILLS DEVELOPMENT

I slept and dreamt that life was joy.
I awoke and saw that life was service.
I acted, and behold, service was joy.
Rabindranath Tagore

The Ritz-Carlton Hotel Company is lauded worldwide for its rich service culture. The hotel's unwavering commitment to service is a true celebration of their customers. Everything that the ladies and gentlemen who work at the hotel do for the ladies and gentlemen who visit their hotel to make their visit unique and memorable comes straight from the heart. When service and service values are so deeply embedded in a company's DNA, it is impossible to contain it within the boundaries of the hotel for the sole benefit of hotel guests. Sooner or later, it will jump the wall and manifest itself as a "force of good" for the communities within which the hotel properties operate.

This is exactly what happened at The Ritz-Carlton. The service culture walked out of the front door and introduced itself as a force of good to the various communities in which the hotel operates in the form of their "Community Footprints" program. The program is an integral part of the hotel company's service values, and is aligned with its long-range plan and business operations. Its logo, a heart formed by footprints, symbolizes the genuine commitment the ladies and gentlemen of The Ritz-Carlton have to their communities, and is merely an extension of the service commitment they have inside the hotel to the ladies and gentlemen who are their guests. Community Footprints projects focus one of three areas—life and career skills for disadvantaged children, care for the environment, and hunger and poverty relief.

The case study that follows involves a program aimed at developing life and career skills among at-risk youth between 14 and 16 years old who attend schools in disadvantaged communities, like inner cities. Called, "Succeed Through Service," the program's primary goal is to encourage and help participating students to stay in school, understand the value of an education, and graduate.

Developed in partnership with America's Promise Alliance, an organization chaired by Mrs. Alma Powell (wife of General Colin L. Powell, founding Chairman of America's Promise) and dedicated to increasing the U.S. national high school graduation rates to 90 percent, Succeed Through Service has benefited over 15,000 students since its launch in 2009, and has been a resounding success, as the following testimonial attests.

"I learned from you why I should follow my passion. You taught me to work hard and how to be successful. I took away your Ritz-Carlton core values and advice to better and further my life. I appreciate all the time and advice that my mentors give to me."

Mathew, Student, Queens Satellite School, New York, USA

How does it work? Employees of The Ritz-Carlton family act as educators and mentors, and provide both a curriculum and an environment for learning and developing job, social, and life skills. The program's three-part hands-on engagement curriculum takes employees into classrooms of disadvantaged community schools, and brings students to The Ritz-Carlton hotels for practical training, which has three parts.

First, the students learn about the workings of the hospitality industry, one of the largest employers globally. They are exposed to a variety of career opportunities ranging from housekeepers, to chefs, to guest relations and hotel managers. For many, this is truly an eye-opener, as their concept of the hospitality industry before walking into the hotel was either non-existent, or limited to jobs in fast-food outlets.

Next, they learn valuable workplace and professional skills, such as the importance of eye-contact, a great smile and a firm handshake, table etiquette, healthy eating habits, grooming, and job interviewing skills.

Finally, all students participate in a capstone project that stresses the importance of giving back to the community. The capstone project also teaches students the importance of presentation skills and the value of teamwork and collaboration.

At the end of the "Succeed Through Service" training, participating students are able to imagine previously unimagined futures, and they leave with valuable life skills that make it more likely for them to achieve those futures.

The Ritz-Carlton offers the "Succeed Through Service" program at properties around the world. While the core curriculum stays unchanged, local hotels do fine-tune and customize the content to fit the pressing needs of their specific communities. For example, The Ritz-Carlton in San Juan, Puerto Rico, the island's first "Green Hotel," modified the last step of the curriculum when working with students from René Marqués Middle School to reflect its extreme passion for the environment.

The first two steps were standard and focused on making students aware of the multitude of career options beyond the limiting occupational stereotypes they may have grown up with, like hair stylist, firefighter, or policeman. The hotel staff facilitated this new awareness and the imagining of vastly different job and career possibilities by sharing their own personal and professional stories.

The capstone project, though, was tied to caring for the environment. Students were taught environmentally-responsible behaviors, with a special focus on reducing electricity consumption, since Puerto Rico has one of the highest incidences of light pollution in the world. The program also emphasized the importance of protecting nature and natural reserves, like the rich coral reef marine reserve—Isla Verde Coral Reef Marine Reserve—which lies in the waters fronting the hotel, and which The Ritz-Carlton is publicly committed to protecting and preserving.

The Community Footprint and Succeed Through Service programs are an impressive testament to The Ritz-Carlton's commitment to increase the wellbeing and prosperity of the communities in which it operates. Equally impressive is the hotel's willingness to share its knowledge and inspire other organizations. Buoyed by the success of its own programs, The Ritz-Carlton has created an open-source, non-proprietary Succeed Through Service toolkit in the hopes that other organizations will also join forces in helping young students complete their education and acquire job and life skills, so they can lead productive lives and have successful careers in professions previously unimagined, or considered out of reach.

TRUE EMPOWERMENT (ECONOMIC, EDUCATIONAL, SOCIAL, NUTRITIONAL)

Let me make the songs for the people
Songs for the young and old...
songs to thrill the hearts of men
With more abundant life....
Our world, so worn and weary,
Needs music, pure and strong...
Frances Ellen Watkins Harper,
Lines from "Songs for the People"

A community that has attracted significant attention in recent years is the "Bottom of the Pyramid (BoP)," the approximately 4 billion people living on less than USD 1,500 per annum (based on purchasing power parity in USD). However, the initial excitement concerning the BoP had little to do with the community's needs, pain, or its problems. The excitement was all about what the community represented, an "untapped resource of incremental revenue and profit." *Fortune* at the BoP is what propelled a large number of companies to action, not a desire to share and redistribute wellbeing and prosperity.

Fortunately, not all organizations perceived the BoP merely as untapped profit potential. Several also saw the BoP as an opportunity to truly empower the community by fundamentally altering the equation of its members with age-old shackles, such as social inequality, lack of earning ability, and poor nutrition. Hindustan Unilever Limited (HUL), a subsidiary of the global giant, Unilever, and India's largest Fast Moving Consumer Goods

Company (FMCG) is one of these organizations. Every day, the company's iconic brands, like Lux, Surf, Lifebuoy, and Lipton, make a significant contribution to enhancing the quality of life of millions of Indian citizens, including those living at the BoP. In recent decades, partly due to its rich history of improving the socio-economic landscape of the communities in which it operates, and partly in response to the changing business ethos of the 21st century, HUL has launched several programs and projects to benefit and empower the BoP community.

One initiative that has inspired several organizations and individuals around the world is Project *Shakti* (Hindi word for power). The project's goal is to lessen the dependence of women in rural areas on wayward husbands and oppressive in-laws, by empowering them economically. It achieves this goal by establishing the women—who frequently are consumers of HUL brands— as distributors for HUL's brands. Called *Shakti Ammas* (literally powerful women, or powerful mothers), the women are now able to liberate themselves financially, thanks to the regular income stream generated by their new enterprises. HUL teaches the *Shakti Ammas* skills necessary for entrepreneurs to run a business, such as basic accounting, selling, and IT. The company augments this training with tangible productivity tools, such as smart phones, that have mini Enterprise Resource Packages (ERPs) pre-loaded on them so the *Shakti Ammas* can run their businesses more efficiently.

In 2010, HUL extended the *Shakti* Entrepreneur Program to include husbands and/or brothers of the *Shakti Ammas*. The male *Shakti* entrepreneurs, called *Shaktimaans* (powerful man), help extend the distribution reach to surrounding villages, as they operate on bicycles and are therefore able to cover larger areas than Shakti *Ammas* can on foot. Today, Project *Shakti* empowers and provides livelihood-enhancing opportunities to nearly 70,000 *Shakti* Entrepreneurs (*Shakti Ammas* + *Shaktimaans*) who distribute HUL Brands in more than 162,000 villages and reach over four million rural households.

Danone, the French multinational corporation dedicated to achieving health through food, implemented something similar in South Africa. They empowered BoP women by training and educating them to become entrepreneurs and distributors of Danimal, an innovative yogurt-based product fortified with nutrients, like Vitamin A, Iron, and Zinc, designed specifically to meet the nutritional shortcomings in the typical diet of children from BoP families. And just like the *Shakti Ammas* in the HUL case above, these women distributors were called "Danimamas" (like the *Shakti Ammas*) and "Daniladies." Unfortunately, Danimal, the brand, couldn't survive the departure of Maria Pretorius, the venture's key champion and sponsor. But, its business model has been replicated on a new brand, Mayo, a yogurt drink available in several flavors, such as banana, pineapple, and mixed fruit.

Simultaneously, Danimal—the yogurt brand—and its business model have been exported *in toto* to Bangladesh. Nobel Laureate Muhammad Yunus and Franck Riboud, CEO of Group Danone, joined hands and launched Grameen Danone, with the mission of producing and selling specially-fortified yogurt to improve the health of Bangladeshi BoP children. And just like Project Shakti and Danimal, the Bangladeshi project also empowers women from the poorest local communities. Called "*Shokti* Ladies" (*Shokti* is also power; *Shakti* in Hindi, *Shokti* in Bengali), these women operate as entrepreneur-distributors for Danimal, which enables them to increase their own wellbeing and prosperity, and that of their immediate families.

ASSET CREATION (HOMES, HOSPITALS)

"The marvel of a house is not that it shelters or warms a man, nor that its walls belong to him. It is that it leaves its trace on language. Let it remain a sign. Let it form, deep in the heart, that obscure range from which, as waters from a spring, are born our dreams."

Antoine de Saint-Exupery
(Author of "The Little Prince")

Barring the perpetually peripatetic, virtually all people from all cultures dream of someday owning a home. Not just for its walls and the shelter it provides, not just for its asset value, but more importantly because homes have a way of giving their owners permission to walk, talk, and think just a tad bit taller and braver.

Homes are the cradles of our dreams. Unfortunately, before a large majority in this world can enter that cradle, there is another more difficult dream they need to fulfill. For millions on this planet, owning a home, even a basic modest home, is often a far-fetched dream, and one that has the potential of turning into a nightmare. Which is what makes Cemex's *Patrimonio Hoy* (Spanish for "Personal Property Today") a world-class role model for how businesses can be a force of good for communities to create the most fundamental and satisfying of all assets—a home.

Headquartered in Mexico, Cemex is one the largest cement and home building supplies companies in the world. The company understood and possessed the basic elements that low-income "do-it-yourself" (DIY) homebuilders need to build a house—materials, technical know-how, and money. But how could it take these traditional skills and assets and help thousands of low-income Mexican families fulfill their dream of building a house?

In a move atypical and uncharacteristic of global behemoths, Cemex embraced the "I am a nobody" philosophy (discussed earlier in the essay on "Ego") and issued a public "Declaration of Ignorance." This freed them to ask, observe, and learn. Consequently, Cemex invested in a unique, large-scale anthropological survey to learn more about the roadblocks and obstacles faced by the low-income families trying to build homes. The study identified four main roadblocks—lack of capital, uneven access to specialized knowledge, unreliable contractors and engineers, and variable quality of materials.

These findings and insights helped Cemex develop *Patrimonio Hoy*, a custom-tailored membership program for fulfilling the unique needs of the low-income DIY Mexican consumer engaged in home building and home improvement. Key features of the program, launched in 2000, are described below.

1. Customers become members of a local Patrimonio Hoy cell in groups of three; the group commits to a 70-week membership, remits a weekly payment of $10-$15, which is held as credit toward future housing material delivery.

2. Materials are delivered in seven installments over the course of the membership.

3. Cemex provides an engineer and architect to facilitate and oversee the construction.

4. The cost of materials remains unchanged for the duration of the project, protecting customers from fluctuations in price and economic conditions.

5. Cemex provides storage of materials in case members run into employment problems, or wish to delay construction.

Patrimonio Hoy operates over 100 Cemex offices in Mexico and has expanded operations to four other countries—Columbia, Nicaragua, Costa Rica, and the Dominican Republic. Since inception, it has provided affordable home improvement solutions to over one million low-income individuals, and encouraged another 350,000 to build their own homes. The program has been honored and recognized by several international awards for promoting sustainable development and fostering the reduction of poverty, most notably the 2006 World Business Award and the 2009 HABITAT Award, both given by the United Nations.

But, Cemex is not stopping here. It is expanding to additional developing countries and integrating social and environmental features into the program, such as raising awareness of climate change, introducing energy efficient appliances, and promoting responsible energy-consumption behaviors.

ALLIANCES AND PARTNERSHIPS

"People are always blaming circumstances for what they are. I don't believe in circumstances. The people who get on in this world are the people who get up and look for the circumstances they want, and, if they can't find them, make them."

George Bernard Shaw

George Bernard Shaw's admonition should be treated with caution and compassion. There are a large number of people in this world who don't have the power or resources to make circumstances they want. Their distress merits our compassion. But not in the case of large, resource rich organizations: blaming circumstances doesn't behoove them. They do have the capacity and ability to script new futures—perhaps not alone, but definitely in partnership and alliances with others.

Many of the world's most urgent problems, especially in the field of public health, are too large and complex for any one entity—individual, organization, community, country—to tackle single-handedly. Malaria is one of them. Based on health statistics published by WHO and individual countries, this public health menace affects close to 2 billion people in over 100 countries. Half of the cases reported globally occur in five African countries: Nigeria, Democratic Republic of Congo (DRC), Ethiopia, Tanzania and Kenya, where in the worst-hit areas, the disease often kills over 500,000 poor people a year. Even though drugs, insecticides, and mosquito nets have helped bring relief to several communities, they have yet to make a significant dent in reducing fatalities among the poor living in remote areas, especially sub-Saharan Africa.

It is an undiluted tragedy because the vast majority of malaria-caused deaths are preventable. The problem is not availability of ACT (Artemisinin-based Combination Therapy), a WHO recommended first-line treatment for uncomplicated malaria, or the knowledge of how to treat the disease. The problem is circumstances, specifically the "last mile." Poor supply-chain management and limited, or non-existent, stock control and disease forecasting procedures often result in ACT being out of stock in local health facilities, even when sufficient stocks are available centrally. If circumstances can be created to remove this imbalance in supply and demand between central and local availability of ACT, then the number of malaria-related deaths can be reduced dramatically.

This is exactly what SMS for Life (SMS—Short Message Service or text message), a Roll Back Malaria partnership initiative launched and led by the global healthcare company Novartis in 2009, set out to accomplish. Fueled by the personal passion, energy, and mission of Jim Barrington, who was then the Chief Information Officer (CIO) of Novartis, SMS for Life is a simple stock taking and inventory communication program to improve anti-malarial drug supply in rural areas and eliminate stock outs. It uses mobile telephones to send and receive messages, and a web-based, Google maps reporting tool to communicate with a central team about inventory levels and stock out possibilities across all health facilities in targeted rural areas.

Initially, according to Barrington in a 2010 article for *Malaria Journal*, the program was rolled out as a 21-week pilot, covering 129 health facilities in three districts of rural Tanzania—Lindi rural, Ulanga, and Kigoma. The program was implemented by a public-private alliance and partnership comprising The Tanzanian

Ministry of Health and Social Welfare (government agency), The Roll Back Malaria Partnership (a WHO-hosted global partnership to fight malaria), Novartis Pharma AG (training and medical resources), Vodafone (telecommunications provider), and IBM (project planning and execution). What is remarkable about this partnership was that it was implemented with *no centralized budget and no formal contracts or memorandum of understanding.* Each commercial partner funded their own activities. The pilot was a resounding success. Out-of-stock positions for the 4 dosage strengths of ACT and quinine injectable fell from 78% in week 1 to 26% in week 21, and the supply of ACT increased by 64% and that of quinine by 36% across all three districts.

Since its inception, SMS for Life 1.0, as the phone-based version is called, has been piloted in over 10,000 Health Care Facilities in several developing countries, like Cameroon, with over 3,000 active facilities. According to the Novartis Malaria Initiative, the next incarnation of the program, SMS for Life 2.0, will be a tablet-based platform, which will have greater connectivity and data collection capabilities, enabling all levels in the health pyramid (districts, regions, national programs, ministry of health) to make fact-based decisions, resulting in more accurate allocation of ACT and resources to meet malaria treatment needs. Discussions concerning its usage are currently underway in Gabon, Nigeria, and Zambia. The program expects that during 2016-2017 5,000 additional health care facilities will benefit from the introduction of SMS for Life 2.0.

Recognized and applauded globally as a landmark social and business innovation, SMS for Life has received numerous awards and recognitions, including the 2012 Ethical Corporation Award for Best Corporate/NGO Partnership, and Computerworld's 21st Century Achievement Award in the Innovation IT category. It is a telling and inspiring example of how, by investing in alliances and partnerships, soulful leaders can create not just the circumstances they desire, but also make the world a better place.

All human journeys begin with a dream.

Sometimes, however, circumstances and resources rob individuals and communities of their dreams. Everything that soulful leaders and their organizations do to help increase the wellbeing and prosperity of the communities in which they operate is about restoring and reigniting dreams.

And more....

Whether it's The Ritz-Carlton investing in communities by teaching poor and disadvantaged school children vital life and job skills, and helping them imagine unimaginable futures of perhaps one day being the General Manager of a Ritz-Carlton hotel...

Whether it's Hindustan Unilever and Danone investing in communities by truly empowering Shakti Ammas, Danimamas, and Shokti Ladies and helping them to become entrepreneurs and start their own micro-distribution businesses...

Whether it's CEMEX helping Latin American communities improve their current homes, or build new ones...

Whether it's Novartis investing in alliances and partnerships to help fight, and perhaps even eradicate, malaria...

Hold fast to dreams
For if dreams die
Life is a broken-winged bird
That cannot fly.
Hold fast to dreams
For when dreams go
Life is a barren field
Frozen with snow.

Langston Hughes, "Dreams"

Soulful leaders hold fast to their dreams of being a force of good, and of making the world a better place. They show courage by first orbiting beyond their own concerns of profit and prosperity. Next they stop to help, and in doing so increase the wellbeing and prosperity of communities in which they live and operate, which then creates circumstances for the individuals living there to have the freedom to dream their own unique dreams. Because before these individuals and communities can imagine alternate realities, before they can hold fast to their own unique dreams, they must first have the ability and means to dream.

THINK ABOUT IT

- Think of your own skills, competencies, and knowledge – your strengths. Which strengths could you leverage to ignite purposeful dreams in the communities surrounding your place of work, and fill your life with meaning?

TALK ABOUT IT

- Is your work group doing enough to be a force of good for the communities surrounding your organization, without sacrificing your own needs for "succeeding and doing well?"

ACT ON IT

- Raise your hand to lead, or be a significant part of an initiative to increase the wellbeing and prosperity of the communities in which your organization lives and operates.

Third Orbit: Planet Earth

Plant a new Truffula. Treat it with care.
Give it clean water. And feed it fresh air.
Grow a forest. Protect it from axes that hack.
Then the Lorax
and all of his friends
may come back.

Dr. Seuss, "The Lorax"

Trust a children's book to remind adults of their obligations to the planet.

I don't remember the first time I read, "The Lorax," but I do remember the last time—just before I started writing this essay. The assonant sounds of fabricated words and portmanteaus grab your ears (a la Jabberwocky), and the illustrations mesmerize your eyes, but it's the years-ahead-of-its-time theme that makes the book a timeless treasure.

(For those who haven't read the book, or have forgotten the story, it involves a crazy-with-greed character called Once-ler, who hacks down Truffula trees to make Thneeds, which are fine somethings—

shirts, socks, gloves, hats—that all people need. Speaking for the trees, The Lorax, an environmentally-responsible character, cautions the Once-ler, who laughs him off. With the help of his relatives, the Once-ler hacks and hacks and makes more and more and more Thneeds, and gets bigger and bigger. Till one day, there are no more trees... and...no more work...and...no more Thneeds; just an empty factory and a bad-smelling sky...and...no more Lorax, who left through a hole in the smog without a trace).

The book and its prescient theme echoes a poem by another vision-ary, William Blake.

The tree which moves some to tears of joy

is in the eyes of others

only a green thing

that stands in the way...

William Blake, Lines from a letter written by the poet-painter

The Truffula tree that moved the Lorax to tears of joy was, for the Once-ler, a mere thing, a consumable source of bright-colored tufts with which he could make Thneeds. His greed for "more" blinded him to a simple truth: that his life was intertwined with that of the Truffula trees. So when greed consumes and kills trees, we eventually consume and kill ourselves too. Once the Once-ler had felled the last Truffula, once there were no more Truffula trees left standing *and* there was no Once-ler either, he had effectively felled himself, his factory, and his Thneed business.

Can this be prevented? Can it be reversed, this destruction of the very resources—trees, water, air—on which our lives depend? It can be. But not until we follow the advice offered by the ending of "The Lorax:

UNLESS someone like you
cares a whole awful lot,
nothing is going to get better.
It's not.
Dr. Seuss, "The Lorax"

The time for caring "a whole awful lot" is here. The time for soulful leaders to make their leadership journeys count toward benefiting the planet, is now. Because while The Lorax may be mere fiction, the cycle of destruction that Dr. Seuss so poetically describes in it is not. It is real and is taking place all around us. The consequences of "not caring a whole awful lot" are dire, as the environmentalist and scientist Bill McKibben warns in "*The End of Nature.*"

"An increase of one degree in average temperature moves the climatic
zones thirty-five to fifty miles north... The trees will die. Consider
nothing more than that – just that the trees will die."
Bill McKibben, "The End of Nature"

Fortunately, all over the globe, many individuals, institutions and organizations do care a whole lot and go to work every day to enhance the planet's wellbeing. Large activist organizations like Greenpeace promote solutions for a greener and more peaceful future through protests and activism. Smaller, more focused organizations like iPrefer30 raise awareness of low temperature washing and more sustainable use of detergents. Fish2fork, an organization focused on sustainable fishing, rates restaurants on the sustainability of seafood featured on their menus. Individuals like Dr. Vandana Shiva, a world-renowned physicist and activist, devotes herself to promoting organic farming and protecting the diversity and integrity of living resources—especially native seeds. This book and I salute them for their relentless, selfless toil. But this essay, as was the case with the essay on communities, is not about these individuals and organizations, whose primary mission is to improve the health of the planet. This essay is about organizations and institutions whose primary business is the production of Thneeds—jeans, detergents, gasoline, carbonated beverages—and the role their leaders can and should play in ensuring that their organizations and leadership journeys act as a "force of good" for the planet. Because the planet is ours to protect, not to ruin.

"We do not inherit the earth from our ancestors
We borrow it from our children."
Native American and Other Early Cultures

And from our children's children, and from all future generations.

At this juncture, some evolutionists and psychologists may rudely remind us that we haven't progressed enough as a species to concern ourselves with the needs of future generations. All we are capable of, they maintain, is obsessing with the immediate, favoring short-term production and consumption over longer-term advantages. Perhaps. But that's why the need for soulful leadership is greater than ever. Even if we concede that soulful leaders can't influence the consumption, utilization, and disposal patterns of their employees, they certainly can and should control how their organizations produce products and services for consumption by the world's population (we'll give Thneeds a rest, and deploy the more conventional expression—products and services). Soulful leaders need to repurpose and refocus their leadership journeys, and chart a sustainable path forward. In concrete terms, this means that the procurement, production, consumption, and waste management processes deployed by their organizations shouldn't exhaust the stock of non-renewable resources.

The phrase, "sustainable development," may be of relatively recent vintage, but the ideas encapsulated within it, like overpopulation, poverty, income inequality…even climate change… aren't; their pedigree goes back several hundred years to thinkers like Malthus and Veblen. This poses a disturbing question: "If the awareness of these problems is not new, why have we continued to harm the planet—exploit and destroy its scarce resources that support and nurture us—at an ever-increasing rate?" The answer is simple, but boorish. As with so many other "nobly intentioned" ideas in the past, everyone "talked a lot," but nobody really "cared a whole awful lot." The values and priorities of countries and organizations pulled them in other directions, and derailed the implementation of programs concerned with the planet's welfare. The planet suffered from the classical tragedy of the commons: The earth "belonged to everybody," and thus "to nobody."

To illustrate, the world's first Earth Summit was held in Rio de Janeiro in 1992. The summit's aims were to obtain global commitment for more enlightened ways of achieving economic development without environmental pollution and destruction of the planet's irreplaceable natural resources. There was abundant global excitement; thousands of people from all walks of life were drawn into the Rio process, and there were scintillating discussions on several critical issues, like fossil fuel alternatives, public transportation, and scarcity of water. Scores of governments and organizations shook hands and agreed to evaluate and redirect their growth policies and plans in terms of environmental impact. But the action that followed didn't match the rhetoric.

Between the idea

And the reality

Between the motion

And the act

Falls the shadow

T.S. Eliot, "The Hollow Men"

No, T.S. Eliot was not grading the Rio summit, though he may as well have been. The Rio+20 report card published in 2012 had a ring as stinging as Eliot's lines from "The Hollow Men;" it awarded the global community an "F," stating that the world as a whole had failed to deliver on its Rio promises.

So it's only fair to ask: Why should we believe things will be different in the future? Has anything changed to give us greater hope that, in the coming years, the same shadow will not fall between the idea and the reality of caring for the planet? There are reasons to be optimistic (fingers crossed). Because while the tide of caring for the planet is still well below the "caring a whole awful lot" ideal, there are indisputable signs it has begun to swell.

Since the 2012 UN Conference on Sustainable Development (also held in Rio, and known as Rio 2012), a renewed and shared global reality has started "*crawling* the talk." This reality recognizes explicitly that environmental problems have a global character, meaning, they are interconnected and part of one giant system. Consequently, they are "OUR" problems, and the survival and prosperity of all countries and people, no matter how privileged or deserving in their own esteem, will be threatened if WE (countries, organizations, and people) continue to produce and consume in ways that cause massive and irreversible harm to the planet and its resources.

Simultaneously, there is also, for the first time, an acknowledgment that this fundamental transformation of production and consumption attitudes and behaviors in favor of the planet's wellbeing can't be achieved without the active collaboration of organizations, both commercial and nonprofit. World bodies like the UN, country governments, and global associations can't get there on their own. Along with goals like climate action, life below water, and responsible consumption and production, The UN's Sustainable Development Goals (UNSDG) initiative lists "global partnerships with the private sector" as one of 17 critical goals for transforming the world. Additionally, as the agency is committed to making significant progress toward achieving these goals by the year 2030, it has called for urgent action to "mobilize, redirect, and unlock the transformative power of private resources" to help the world meet the objectives of UNSDG initiative.

Soulful leaders of both large global organizations and smaller organizations operating locally can contribute to UNSDG goals by building organizational cultures and reshaping business operations that care a whole lot more for the health and wellbeing of the planet. Several have already begun nudging their leadership journeys in the direction of greater stewardship of planetary needs, as the following examples illustrate.

Unilever is the world's largest buyer of palm oil. If not sourced responsibly, large-scale usage of palm oil results in extensive deforestation, which increases greenhouse gas emissions, which in turn poses a significant climate change threat. Being the proverbial elephant in the forest, Unilever can't countenance this essential commodity as a source of deforestation and planet degradation. Consequently, in collaboration with other companies and non-profit organizations like Consumer Goods Forum, Tropical Forest Alliance 2020, and the New York Declaration on Forests, Unilever has committed to eliminating deforestation caused by its supply chains, ideally by 2020, which will contribute significantly to UNSDG meeting its "Life On Land" goal (goal number 15). With this end in mind, Unilever has launched several initiatives aimed at sustainably sourcing palm oil for the long-term, such as making its purchases fully traceable and certified sustainable, trading only with organizations and geographies committed to no deforestation, and partnering with governments to embed no-deforestation pledges into national and international policies.

Like Unilever, Levi Strauss & Company (LS&Co.) is also an elephant, albeit in a different jungle, the denim and apparel jungle. LS&Co. also faces a critical sustainability challenge since the apparel industry is a heavy guzzler of water—an extremely scarce resource—at all stages of production and consumption, from growing cotton to manufacturing apparel, to consumer care and home laundry. Realizing this, the company has promised the global community that it will reduce water usage across the entire life-cycle of its products, and use 100 percent sustainable cotton in its operations by 2020 by doing more business with Better Cotton Initiative (BCI) farmers who use up to 18 percent less water than non-BCI farmers in comparable locations. The company is also experimenting with producing more jeans with recycled cotton, since jeans crafted with at least 15 percent recycled cotton use significantly less water during the manufacturing process. Finally, as cotton is grown in some of the most arid regions in the world, LS&Co. is partnering with the World Wildlife Fund to reduce the water impact of its apparel factories located in the water basins of some of the most high-risk countries, such as Bangladesh, Pakistan, Mexico and China. Finally, the company is experimenting with innovative fabric finishing techniques, like Water<Less™, which can save up to 96% of the water in the denim finishing process. Since launching the Water<Less™ processes in 2011, the company has saved more than 1 billion liters of water in the manufacturing of LS&Co. brands.

What's even more encouraging is that it's not just global giants which are responding to calls for sustainable development, even small companies that are not household names are answering the call to contribute to the health and wellbeing of the planet. "The Bark House at Highland Craftsman, Inc," is one such company. The company handcrafts interior and exterior wall coverings from reclaimed Appalachian wood waste using processes that not only express the company's rich heritage of artisanal craftsmanship, but also form an authentic connection between nature, individuals, and the built environment. As Chris McCurry, co-founder of Bark House, explains, "It's not just about creating beautiful buildings, but also about building community beautifully."

For its commitment to sustainable forestry, Bark House was recognized and honored as "**Best for the World**" in 2015 in the environment category by B-Corp, a non-profit organization that certifies companies as a force-for-good if they meet rigorous standards of social and environmental performance, accountability, and transparency. In addition, the company's exterior poplar siding also received the first-ever Cradle to Cradle Certified™ PLATINUM product award. Applauding Bark House, William McDonough, founder of Cradle to Cradle®, said:

"If you look at what's going on at Highland Craftsmen... you are looking at a product that is almost a sacred thing... People are being honored with jobs, forests are being honored with sustainable forestry, and the buildings that use these materials are being honored with safe, healthy materials."

Finally, and equally encouraging as the examples of Unilever, Levi's, Philips, and Bark House, is the growth of global public-private collaborations, like the UN Global Compact and Impact 2030, that are attempting to rally organizations around the world—big and small—to step up and contribute to the achievement of UNSDG goals, and consequently to improve the health and wellbeing of the planet.

However, even as the preceding examples and case studies deserve applause, they are not enough. The planet needs more "caring" than what the companies and non-profits already in the ring can provide. If ever "there was a tide in the affairs of the planet," to paraphrase Shakespeare's Brutus, it is now. Soulful leaders, regardless of the size, scope, and brand-name appeal of their organizations, must repurpose their leadership journeys and make sustainability a way of life. Their role doesn't end there, though. They also need to assume the mantle of "planet ambassadors," not wait for an invitation, so they can educate and inspire other leaders and organizations still sitting on the fence. There are 17 UNSDGs. Helping implement at least one fully should be an obsession for all leaders and their organizations. We—the people of this planet—have made promises to protect the planet and prevent it from degradation in the past, but we haven't always been scrupulous about honoring them. This time we need to ensure a different outcome. Because now we have both awareness and knowledge of how our actions can hurt the planet and the wellbeing of future generations. There are no excuses to justify inaction. In fact, we could consider apathy complicity, abetting degradation of the planet.

> *And thus I clothe my naked villainy*
> *With odd old ends stol'n out of holy writ;*
> *And seem a saint, when most I play the devil.*
> **William Shakespeare, "Richard III"**

This is no time to play the devil with the health of the planet. If anything, we need to upgrade our promises to commitments, because eventually we will have to return the planet we borrowed to the next generation. What then? How will we answer them when looking at what we are returning, they shake their head, look us in the eye, and sigh: "What was your excuse, Mummy, what was your excuse, Daddy?" The truth is we have none. There can be no more urgent agenda for soulful leaders than protecting and preserving the planet.

A very significant global event occurred on May 26, 2016. Norway became the first country in the world to officially ban clear-cutting of trees, fulfilling a pledge it made at the U.N. Climate Summit in 2014. Any product that contributes to deforestation—notably the rainforest—will not be used in the Scandinavian country.

Norway's action resonates forcefully with how "the tree" has featured in this essay. The essay began with the story of The Lorax, and the tragedy of the Truffula trees. The tree is a metaphor for life—*our* lives, life *on* the planet, and life *of* the planet. When the last Truffula tree was felled, life as The Lorax and the Onceler knew it, also ended. The Unilever case study on palm oil also reinforces the importance of trees to the ongoing health of our planet. As Blake reminded us earlier in this essay, trees are more than mere green things.

Consequently, the lines of poetry that follow have one shared focus—to create within us an inner awakening to nurture and protect trees. Because trees are at once a metaphor and a reality: they are a metaphor for life, and they are life. Without trees, life would be unimaginable.

The poplars are felled, farewell to the shade
And the whispering sound of the cool colonnade:
The winds play no longer and sing in the leaves,
Nor Ouse on his bosom their image receives.
(The river Ouse unable to receive the image/reflection of the poplars
on its bosom/surface)
Twelve years have elapsed since I first took a view
Of my favourite field, and the bank where they grew,
And now in the grass behold they are laid,
And the tree is my seat that once lent me a shade.
William Cowper, Lines from, "The Poplar Field"

And if we want the planet to keep its trees, we need to deny ourselves Thneeds, or insist that our Thneeds be made sustainably, so we can restrain the power and dominion we wrongly exercise over trees.

When I consider how
a man-made shift in climate of a few degrees
reveals the rebel power we now
have learned to cultivate
in order to subdue the animals
and take dominion, like a curse,
over the fields, the forests, and the atmosphere —
as if the universe
belonged to us alone – I wonder
if consideration of the family of trees
might give us pause
and let us once again obey the sun,
whose light commands all human laws.

Robert Pack, Lines From "The Trees Will Die"

But the only way we can prevent a shift of *a few degrees* in temperature, and man-made climate change, is if we "re-cognize" the earth (see the earth again with wondrous eyes, as if for the first time), and "rethink" our relationship with it, so that the earth belongs to everybody, and is also everybody's responsibility.

I know the sap that courses through the trees

As I know the blood that flows in my veins.

We are part of the earth and it is part of us.

The earth does not belong to us. We belong to the earth.

The earth is our mother.

What befalls the earth befalls all the sons and daughters

of the earth.

We did not weave the web of life,

We are merely a strand in it.

Whatever we do to the web, we do to ourselves.

Chief Seattle, Lines from, "Brother Eagle, Sister Sky"

Soulful leaders can play an invaluable role in modeling behaviors that communicate, unequivocally, the wisdom of Chief Seattle's words. If they can help the people and organizations they lead genuinely believe that the planet is not merely a means for constantly increasing consumption, and that whatever harms the planet also harms us, then they and their organizations would have taken a giant step in contributing mightily to the future wellbeing and health of this planet.

THINK ABOUT IT

- Think of least 3 personal behaviors and 3 work-related behaviors that you can change to gift a healthier planet to those in queue to inherit it from us.

TALK ABOUT IT

- Talk about how you and your colleagues can "be a force of good" for the planet, by changing personal and work-related behaviors that can materially improve the health and wellbeing of our planet.

ACT ON IT

- Next, as an individual and as a group, change at least one behavior—personal or work-related—so you and your colleagues can gift a healthier planet to those waiting to inherit it from us.

FARING FORWARD…

Epilogue:
Extending The Invitation

Ring the bell that still can ring
Forget your perfect offering
There is a crack in everything
That's how the light gets in
Leonard Cohen, "Anthem"

When Leo Tolstoy, a privileged aristocrat, came face-to-face with the pain and suffering of poverty in the Moscow of his time, he asked a simple, but extremely profound question concerning moving beyond experiencing reality, to reshaping it: "What Then Must We Do?" Perhaps many readers, having reached this point in the journey charted by this book, are asking the same question, albeit in connection with leaders and leadership: "What then must we do?"

So Krishna, as when he admonished Arjuna
On the field of battle...
Not fare well.
But fare forward, voyagers.
T.S. Eliot, "The Dry Salvages; Four Quartets"

The book began with the Prologue extending a simple invitation to readers to explore the **world of Soulful Leadership** with the help of a different set of teachers, the sagely **world of immortal poems**. The motivation for extending that invitation stems from an unshakable conviction that the worldviews and behaviors of many of today's leaders are inadequate to meet what's required for the wellbeing and prosperity of the disparate and conflicting constituencies of today's complex world. For those worldviews and behaviors to transform, leaders and leadership need a new narrative focused not on what leadership is, or who leaders are, but on what leaders and leadership should stand for—a public platform for increasing the wellbeing and prosperity of the greater many, not just the privileged few. Accordingly, this epilogue would like to extend the appeal presented at the end of each essay...Think (about it), Talk (about it), and Act (on it)...and urge readers to make embracing, adopting, and enacting Soulful Leadership ideas and practices an urgent priority in their immediate spheres of life, both work and non-work.

At this stage, regardless of the strength and intensity of one's resolve, it's possible that some readers may find themselves doubting their readiness to act, doubting their readiness to leap, to risk practicing soulful leadership, much like the protégés Apollinaire was trying to coax to the edge in the poem below (also featured in the essay on Risk).

"Come to the edge," he said. "We can't, we're afraid!" they responded.

"Come to the edge," he said. "We can't, we will fall!" they responded.

"Come to the edge," he said.

And so they came. And he pushed them. And they flew.

Christopher Logue

Ready, or not, is a relative state. Many of life's journeys would never begin, or would be aborted shortly after conception, if the sole criteria were the traveler's readiness. Some of the world's most admired and respected leaders were not "ready" or "leader-like" when they were first invited to step on the leadership stage – Mahatma Gandhi, Nelson Mandela, Ratan Tata, Steve Jobs, Bill Gates, A.G. Lafley, and the list goes on. But they took the first step…and another…and another, and every step they took made them more ready. Exactly as Leonard Cohen urges us to do in "Anthem," the song featured at the top of this essay. We must ring the bell, cracks and all, because that's how the light will get in. We must act on the ideas of Soulful Leadership, regardless of how ready, or unready, we may perceive ourselves to be for undertaking this journey, because every step we take will help us become better at practicing Soulful Leadership, and will simultaneously make us more ready to practice it in the future.

Further, *ready* doesn't mean ready across the board, in all aspects and on all dimensions of Soulful Leadership. *Ready* merely means willing to travel, and risk failure, and not turn back, no matter what the demands of the journey. It's quite likely that some leaders may be capable of Soulful Leadership with respect to "Perseverance," but fall short on "Perspective" or "Ego." Additionally, even where leaders are ready (or not ready), context and circumstances intervene causing variations in Soulful Leadership behaviors. For instance, leaders who come from the supply-side of the business may pass the perseverance test involving manufacturing or technology undertakings, but may be less willing to persevere in areas and domains they either can't relate to or don't understand, such as customer behavior and social media marketing.

Finally, a state of readiness to embrace and practice soulful leadership is not reserved just for the chosen few. No leader, no matter how exalted or larger-than-life, has a lock on Soulful Leadership for all times, across all occasions. Not even saints. Even Mother Teresa, now St. Teresa of Calcutta, had people crying foul, accusing her of unfairly sacrificing others to meet her own mission's needs. Exceedingly budget conscious and known for her "haggling prowess," she invariably beat down the prices charged by small vendors who supplied her mission with daily provisions, like potatoes, vegetables, and rice, thereby eroding their already wafer thin margins, and hence their livelihood.

Wislawa Szymborska, the Noble Prize winning Polish poet, approaches the question of whether anybody has a lock on Soulful Leadership behaviors—at all times, across all occasions—in an intriguingly unconventional way in her poem, "A Few Words On The Soul." The entire poem is presented so readers can experience and enjoy the poet's full range of playful seriousness.

We have a soul at times.
No one's got it non-stop,
for keeps.

Day after day,
year after year
may pass without it.

Sometimes
it will settle for awhile
only in childhood's fears and raptures.
Sometimes only in astonishment
that we are old.

It rarely lends a hand
in uphill tasks,
like moving furniture,
or lifting luggage,
or going miles in shoes that pinch.

It usually steps out
whenever meat needs chopping
or forms have to be filled.

For every thousand conversations
it participates in one,
if even that,
since it prefers silence.

Just when our body goes from ache to pain,
it slips off-duty.

It's picky:
it doesn't like seeing us in crowds,
our hustling for a dubious advantage
and creaky machinations make it sick.

Joy and sorrow
aren't two different feelings for it.
It attends us
only when the two are joined.

We can count on it
when we're sure of nothing
and curious about everything.
Among the material objects

it favors clocks with pendulums
and mirrors, which keep on working
even when no one is looking.

It won't say where it comes from
or when it's taking off again,
though it's clearly expecting such questions.

We need it
but apparently
it needs us
for some reason too.

Wislawa Szymborska, "A Few Words on the
Soul," (translated from Polish by Stanislaw
Baranczak and Clare Cavanagh)

Finally, since the need for Soulful Leadership in all aspects of our society today is compelling and crucial, the question concerning being *ready* may be irrelevant. Every day, regardless of continent, country, or industry, we hear the crying need for more Soulful Leadership. Whether it's the Princess Cruise Lines deliberately polluting the oceans and intentionally covering up its crime; or the Modi government demonetizing the INR 500 and 1000 currency notes in India without a comprehensive plan for substituting the old currency with new notes; or Donald Trump and his supporters wanting to "Make America Great Again" at the expense of minorities and certain religious factions; or Brexit and its touted benefits; or the digital transformation of the workplace leading to fewer jobs for humans, we observe the sacrifice framework at play. In each case, the wellbeing and prosperity of some factions of society are sacrificed, and the wellbeing and prosperity of other factions are maintained, or even increased. The question is not whether the sacrifice is right or wrong—this book has eschewed the moralist trap from the outset and will not be seduced into it now. Since sacrifices are inherent in all leadership decisions, the only pertinent question is what's informing and influencing them? Are leaders willfully exploiting the assets they control—people and resources—to feed their self-interests, or are the sacrifices governed by an inner awakening that spawns a sincere desire to increase the wellbeing and prosperity of the greatest many?

Like the tale of the Good Samaritan, all that matters is that we ask ourselves, "Can we afford not to embrace the ideas and practice of soulful leadership?" This book, and the author, are certain the answer is "NO." Not because we want to "...look too good, or talk too wise.... (borrowing a line from Kipling's, "If")." Because, when all the story is finished, someone...perhaps, we ourselves...will ask, "What's the news?" How then will we answer?

When all that story's finished, what's the news?
W.B. Yeats, Line from, "The Choice"

"What's the news?" "What then are we to do?" The questions are simple, the answers exceedingly complex.

This book and its author have had their say, and must exit the stage. It's your turn now, dear reader; the answer is up to you. Thank you for accepting the invitation extended by the Prologue, thank you for journeying this far. The book and I sincerely hope you will continue faring forward, travel even further. The world of Soulful Leadership awaits.

Namaste!

A Request

FROM THE PROLOGUE

"I am acutely aware that an ideal pairing of soulful leadership characteristics and immortal poems is extremely difficult—if not impossible—to achieve.: There will always be soulful leadership characteristics that readers feel should have been included, or omitted. Similarly, with poems: some readers may be disappointed at the omission of a poem, and others with the inclusion of one. My apologies to all such readers in advance. But disappointment needn't cause despair. The last section will suggest opportunities for readers to expand the journey that this book has started. There is room for more."

T.S. Eliot once famously declared that, "poems belong to the reader, not to the poet who wrote the poem," because readers take the poem where they want to take it.

Similarly, every reader's journey with this book is unique, even though the book they read is the same. Readers from around the world, and I, are keen on hearing about your unique journey. Which topics, poems, and calls to action (Think about it, Talk about it, Act on it) resonated most with you? Perhaps there are topics you think should have been included, but were not. Or poems. Or you know of poems that better illuminate the nature and dynamics of soulful leadership. Or both. Perhaps you have stories to tell of your own experiments with soulful leadership. Or you have ideas on how its practice can be encouraged and disseminated. A request – whatever your thoughts, ideas, and experiences, please don't keep them to yourself. Please visit **www.soulfulleadership.world**, and share them with the global community of soulful leadership advocates and enthusiasts. Your sharing will make a difference.

Thank you.

ACKNOWLEDGMENTS AND PERMISSIONS

What they undertook to do
They brought to pass;
W.B. Yeats, "Gratitude To The Unknown Instructors"

ACKNOWLEDGMENTS

Yes, certainly, gratitude to the unknown instructors and their gifts of silent education. And, the known instructors as well – the kindred souls who breathed life into this book through their gifts of time, attention, ideas, caring, and love. I would like to express gratitude for what they brought to pass.

First, two individuals who played the role of teacher, critic, and cheerleader, and who worked hard to keep my content and intentions lively and honest. Heartfelt and sincere appreciation for their advice, critique, and guidance. The book is richer for their involvement and contributions, and for their willingness to stay with it till the end.

- Betty Sue Flowers, Ph.D., poet, business consultant, and Professor Emeritus at the University of Texas, Austin, thank you for believing in me, and encouraging me to explore and dig deeper in search of my own voice and convictions. Thank you also for your honest and candid feedback, and for suggesting different directions and destinations than I had considered. Above all, thank you for your kindness and generosity when the climb got steeper and the oxygen rare.

- Leslee Johnson, poet, philosopher, and creative writing expert, thank you also for believing in me and my venture, and for your unwavering support. Thank you for your in-depth research, and for helping me think of the book's themes and content from the reader's perspective.

Gratitude also to Chris Llewellyn, an award winning poet who I have worked with since the early 1990s, for sharing her vast knowledge of poets and poetry with me. And for her sincere curiosity in the book's primary theme—Soulful Leadership—which, on numerous occasions, emboldened me to travel even further from shore than I had planned.

Next, two visual artists, Vallika Verma and Joan Cox, who helped add an ethereal vibration to the text with their sketches.

- Vallika Verma, a rising, iconoclastic artist, for nudging me in the direction of minimalism, as we brainstormed content and concepts with the help of her pencil drawings.

- Joan Cox, for making those minimalist ideas come to life through a rare combination of listening, experimentation, and artistic skill. Deep thanks to Joan for her willingness to step out of her comfort zone and work with me in a way she never had previously—creating sketches rich in symbolism and meaning, based on the essence of a few select lines of poetry.

Gratitude also to Vrinda Sood, the graphic artist who designed the cover of my novel (The Curse and the Cup), for creating the initial versions of this book's cover.

Next, heartfelt thanks and hearty applause to Justin Sachs, CEO of Motivational Press, and his dedicated team for shepherding this book from idea to reality. Thank you, Justin, for admitting me into your publishing firm's author family, and for the full range of onstage and backstage support involved in finishing the book's cover, designing the website, content editing, and the interior design and layout of the book. A hearty round of applause to your team of specialists.

Sincere thanks also to the publishing houses and their agents for granting me permission to reprint poems and excerpts. Their generosity has made the reading experience richer and more stimulating.

Finally, buckets of gratitude to a band of loving, nurturing, and giving individuals—family, close friends, and committed colleagues—who day in and day out sustained and energized me, and added more stamina and horsepower to my efforts by converting "I into We and Us." They know who they are. Since they are an integral part of my life, I will communicate my deep and sincere gratitude to each of them individually and uniquely. I believe that's what Love would do.

Thank you, all, again and again. All you undertook, you did bring to pass. Heartfelt GRATITUDE for that.

PERMISSIONS

"Leavings, 2005, Number 12," Copyright © 2010 by Wendell Berry, from *Leavings*. Reprinted by permission of Counterpoint.

"Ars Poetica?" [excerpts of 8 l.] from THE COLLECTED POEMS 1931-1987 by CZESLAW MILOSZ. Copyright © 1988 by Czeslaw Milosz Royalties, Inc. Reprinted by permission of HarperCollins Publishers.

Rumi poems reprinted by permission from Coleman Barks.

"No doubt about it," from THE ESSENTIAL HAIKU: VERSIONS OF BASHO, BUSON & ISSA, EDITED WITH AN INTRODUCTION by ROBERT HASS. Introduction and selection copyright © by Robert Hass. Reprinted by permission of HarperCollins Publishers.

"No doubt about it," Issa, translated by Robert Hass, *The Essential Haiku* (Bloodaxe Books, 2013; www.bloodaxebooks.com)

"In Broken Images," by Robert Graves, from "The Complete Poems In One Volume." Reprinted by permission from Carcanet Press Limited.

"To be of use" from CIRCLES ON THE WATER by Marge Piercy, copyright © 1982 by Middlemarsh, Inc. Used by permission of Alfred A. Knopf, an imprint of the Knopf Doubleday Publishing Group, a division of Penguin Random House LLC. All rights reserved.

"Dreams," by Langston Hughes, from "The Complete Poems of Langston Hughes." Reprinted by permission of Harold Ober Associates, Incorporated.

"Dreams" from THE COLLECTED POEMS OF LANGSTON HUGHES by Langston Hughes, edited by Arnold Rampersad with David Roessel, Associate Editor, copyright © 1994 by the Estate of Langston Hughes. Used by permission of Alfred A. Knopf, an imprint of the Knopf Doubleday Publishing Group, a division of Penguin Random House LLC. All rights reserved.

Excerpt(s) from THE LORAX by Dr. Seuss, ® and copyright © by Dr. Seuss Enterprises, L.P. 1971, renewed 1999. Used by permission of Random House Children's Books, a division of Penguin Random House LLC. All rights reserved.

Excerpt(s) from SAND AND FOAM by Kahlil Gibran, copyright © 1926 by Kahlil Gibran, copyright renewed 1954 by Administrators C.T.A of Kahlil Gibran Estate and Mary G. Gibran. Used by permission of Alfred A. Knopf, an imprint of Knopf Doubleday Publishing Group, a division of Penguin Random House LLC. All rights reserved.

"On Self-Knowledge" from THE PROPHET by Kahlil Gibran, copyright © 1923 by Kahlil Gibran, copyright renewed 1951 by Administrators C.T.A of Kahlil Gibran Estate and Mary G. Gibran. Used by permission of Alfred A. Knopf, an imprint of Knopf Doubleday Publishing Group, a division of Penguin Random House LLC. All rights reserved.

"A Few Words on the Soul," by Wislawa Szymborska, from *"MONOLOGUE OF A DOG."* Reprinted by permission of Houghton Mifflin Harcourt.

About the Author

GAURAV BHALLA is a globally recognized thinker-doer who delivers insight-packed experiences that inspire, entertain, and motivate next-day executive action through his training, speaking, consulting, and coaching services.

Committed to helping organizations and individuals Learn, Act, Grow, he has worked with clients like, GSK, Citi, MetLife, Caterpillar, Maersk, Deloitte, and Marriott, and with leading business schools like Georgetown, Duke, Singapore Management University, University of Maryland, GIBS-South Africa, Indian School of Business. In recognition of his proven experience and stellar reputation, he was awarded the "2016 Executive Education Specialist of the Year" award, by Corporate Vision, a UK-based global media company.

A committed writer, he writes business books and articles, poems, novels, and screenplays. What sets Gaurav apart from other professionals and writers like him is his *growth mindset* and his *purpose that values the humanity of individuals more than their executive brilliance.* Meet him at www.gauravbhalla.com, and learn more about the book at www.soulfulleadershipworld.com.

CPSIA information can be obtained
at www.ICGtesting.com
Printed in the USA
BVOW06s0359300717

490178BV00011B/13/P